THE SKEPTIC DISPOSITION IN CONTEMPORARY CRITICISM

PRINCETON ESSAYS IN LITERATURE

For a list of titles in the series,
see pages 189-91

THE SKEPTIC DISPOSITION

IN CONTEMPORARY CRITICISM

Eugene Goodheart

PRINCETON UNIVERSITY PRESS

Published by Princeton University Press, 41 William Street,
Princeton, New Jersey 08540
In the United Kingdom: Princeton University Press,
Guildford, Surrey

Library of Congress Cataloging in Publication Data will be
found on the last printed page of this book

ISBN 0-691-06626-4

Publication of this book has been aided by the
Henry A. Laughlin Fund of Princeton University Press

This book has been composed in Linotron Baskerville
with Linotron Cheltenham display

Clothbound editions of Princeton University Press books
are printed on acid-free paper, and binding materials are
chosen for strength and durability. Paperbacks, although
satisfactory for personal collections, are not usually suitable
for library rebinding

Printed in the United States of America
by Princeton University Press
Princeton, New Jersey

In Memory of

MY FATHER SAMUEL

(1900-1981)

CONTENTS

ACKNOWLEDGMENTS ix

INTRODUCTION 3

1. Criticism at the Present Time 16
2. The Transcendental Site: From Heaven to Earth 39
3. Roland Barthes and the Monster of Totality 56
4. Reading with/out a Text 88
5. Discourse without Foundation 111
6. A Question of Meaning 136
7. Literature as Play 155

CONCLUSION: Deconstruction and Social Criticism 173

INDEX 181

ACKNOWLEDGMENTS

I do not know whether I adequately met the objections of my friends who read the book in manuscript. But I am immensely grateful to them for having helped make the book stronger and more persuasive than it was before they read it. Daniel Aaron, Joan Bamberger, Alvin Kibel, Robert Nozick, Ben L. Reid, Marc Shell, Alan Trachtenberg, and Theodore Weiss proved to me that each reading is at once subjective and objective and that even intellectual differences depend upon shareable meanings and values. Thanks are also due to The National Endowment for the Humanities for granting me a fellowship in 1980-81 for work on this book. I would like to acknowledge the permission to reprint material from earlier versions of chapters, which appeared in various journals. Chapter 1 appeared in *Critical Inquiry* (March 1983), a publication of The University of Chicago Press as "Arnold at the Present Time"; Chapter 3 as "The Myths of Roland," in *Partisan Review* 2 (1980); Chapter 4 as "The Text and the Interpretive Community," in *Daedalus* (Winter 1983); and Chapter 7 as "Literature as a Game," in *TriQuarterly* (Fall 1981), a publication of Northwestern University.

I want to express my appreciation to Wade Rollins and Arlyne Weisman for their patient cunning in deciphering and typing the manuscript and to Nick Humez for his careful and perceptive work on the index.

Waltham, Massachusetts
March 1984

ACKNOWLEDGMENTS

I do not know whether I adequately met the objections of my friends who read the book in manuscript. But I am immensely grateful to them for having helped make the book stronger and more persuasive than it was before they read it. Daniel Aaron, Joan Bamberger, Alvin Kibel, Robert Nozick, Ben L. Reid, Marc Shell, Alan Trachtenberg, and Theodore Weiss proved to me that each reading is at once subjective and objective and that even intellectual differences depend upon shareable meanings and values. Thanks are also due to The National Endowment for the Humanities for granting me a fellowship in 1980-81 for work on this book. I would like to acknowledge the permission to reprint material from earlier versions of chapters, which appeared in various journals. Chapter 1 appeared in *Critical Inquiry* (March 1983), a publication of The University of Chicago Press as "Arnold at the Present Time"; Chapter 3 as "The Myths of Roland," in *Partisan Review* 2 (1980); Chapter 4 as "The Text and the Interpretive Community," in *Daedalus* (Winter 1983); and Chapter 7 as "Literature as a Game," in *TriQuarterly* (Fall 1981), a publication of Northwestern University.

I want to express my appreciation to Wade Rollins and Arlyne Weisman for their patient cunning in deciphering and typing the manuscript and to Nick Humez for his careful and perceptive work on the index.

Waltham, Massachusetts
March 1984

ACKNOWLEDGMENTS

I do not know whether I adequately met the objections of my friends who read the book in manuscript. But I am immensely grateful to them for having helped make the book stronger and more persuasive than it was before they read it. Daniel Aaron, Joan Bamberger, Alvin Kibel, Robert Nozick, Ben L. Reid, Marc Shell, Alan Trachtenberg, and Theodore Weiss proved to me that each reading is at once subjective and objective and that even intellectual differences depend upon shareable meanings and values. Thanks are also due to The National Endowment for the Humanities for granting me a fellowship in 1980-81 for work on this book. I would like to acknowledge the permission to reprint material from earlier versions of chapters, which appeared in various journals. Chapter 1 appeared in *Critical Inquiry* (March 1983), a publication of The University of Chicago Press as "Arnold at the Present Time"; Chapter 3 as "The Myths of Roland," in *Partisan Review* 2 (1980); Chapter 4 as "The Text and the Interpretive Community," in *Daedalus* (Winter 1983); and Chapter 7 as "Literature as a Game," in *TriQuarterly* (Fall 1981), a publication of Northwestern University.

I want to express my appreciation to Wade Rollins and Arlyne Weisman for their patient cunning in deciphering and typing the manuscript and to Nick Humez for his careful and perceptive work on the index.

Waltham, Massachusetts
March 1984

THE SKEPTIC DISPOSITION IN CONTEMPORARY CRITICISM

Scepticism is a highly civilised trait, though, when it declines into pyrrhonism, it is one of which civilisation can die. Where scepticism is strength, pyrrhonism is weakness: for we need not only the strength to defer a decision, but the strength to make one.

—T. S. Eliot

INTRODUCTION

Until recently theory occupied an uncertain place in literary study. The New Criticism taught us how to read individual works of literature. Its theory consisted of heuristic concepts like paradox and ambiguity (concepts that told us what to look for). It cautioned against certain fallacies in reading, for example, the intentional fallacy, which mistakes the source of meaning in the author's intentions or the affective fallacy, which confuses the reader's private emotional associations with the feelings evoked by the work. To say this is to be unfair to the achievements of I. A. Richards and Kenneth Burke, but I am more concerned with the way theory was perceived and used in the profession at large than with the intrinsic character of specific theories. Theory was (and remember I am speaking in the past tense) a kind of speculation about constraints in order to make practical criticism a disciplined activity. The primary—for many the exclusive—activity of literary study since the beginning of the New Criticism has been the interpretation of texts. In fact, once the New Criticism had established itself, it became possible to discount the value of literary theory altogether. T. S. Eliot, the unwilling father of New Criticism, had declared that the one thing needful was intelligence. F. R. Leavis pronounced himself against literary theory (and with increasing vehemence toward the end of his long career). For Eliot and Leavis, theory meant abstraction, method, system: terms denoting states of mind obnoxious to the literary intelligence, to which Matthew Arnold attributed "flexibility, perceptiveness, and judgment." This view of literary intelligence is Arnold's abiding legacy to the New Criticism, whatever else of his legacy it may have renounced. Though I speak of the past, the antitheoretical animus of the New Criticism persists in certain English critics who can't resist a sneer every time they utter the word "theory."

The theoretical impulse, however, was never wholly extinct. The largely negative achievement of the Chicago Aristotelians was in their demonstration of confusion and inadequacy in New Critical theory and practice. In particular, the Aristotelians found the New Critics wanting in a conception of literary structure. The remedy lay in the theory of genres. The principal element of structure was plot, which could be discovered even in a lyric poem. For the New Critics structure implied system and rigidity. They could afford to ignore the Aristotelians, because Aristotelian speculation was for the most part arrested in a servile piety toward the master's texts.[1]

But the advent of Northrop Frye was another matter. Frye, too, was inspired by Aristotle's theory of genres, but he was not slavish in his use of the theory. *Anatomy of Criticism* is an astonishing work of theoretical construction, bold in its conception and ingenious in its detail. Frye went beyond Aristotle to create new tasks for criticism and scholarship. The goal of criticism was no longer the isolated understanding of individual works of literature. The critic could now discover the generic or modal features of a work with a view toward understanding its place in the structure of literature as a whole. Frye's work had enormous authority for a while.

Ironically, it lost some of that authority when structuralism (a European import) came on the scene. I say ironically, because one might expect structuralism to provide reinforcement for Frye's work. Like Frye, structuralism (in the work of Barthes, Todorov, and Genette) promised a

[1] There are, of course, exceptions. Wayne Booth's *Rhetoric of Fiction* (Chicago: University of Chicago Press, 1961) is a magisterial work that transcends the school.

science of literary understanding in the study of the structures of literature. I suspect that the reason for the overshadowing of Frye by structuralism was that Frye, unlike the structuralists, remains a traditional humanist. If he distinguishes between the scientific understanding of literature and the experience of it, his practice as a critic happily fails to decontaminate his discourse of questions of value. The structuralists, on the other hand, fully prepared "to commit a social science," are more rigorous than Frye in excluding value judgments from literary study.

In any event, for some serious students of literature, both Frye and the structuralists promised the possibility of creating a body of knowledge that would give to literary study the dignity of a discipline for the first time in its history. No other field in the humanities or the social sciences would tolerate the amateurishness and amorphousness that characterized literary study. Theory would have to occupy a central place. It would now inspire the work of practical criticism and scholarship as it never had done before. In fact, the relationship between theory and practice under the aegis of structuralism would be the reverse of what it had been under the New Criticism. In the New Criticism, theory remained in the background, as a tactful regulator of the activity of practical criticism. In structuralism, theory created the tasks and defined the procedures for practical criticism. And the most important difference was that structuralism changed or tried to change the goal of literary study from the interpretation of the meanings of literary works to the knowledge of the conditions of meaning. In an essay "The Critical Assumption," Jonathan Culler, perhaps the most lucid advocate of structuralism, declares the interpretation of texts to be an insidious activity that must be transcended. Culler speaks of replacing interpretation with "studies of the relationship between literary discourse and other forms of discourse, literature's relationship to the world, the role of fictions in the psychic economies of readers and writers, the operation of transference involved in reading." He proposes the following example:

> Suppose that someone were interested in the problem of *catharsis*, a notion which has often figured in definitions of the tragic genre and which makes claims about the effect of fictions in the mental economies of readers and thus about the relationship between literature and "life." This is an interesting question and to elucidate it would, I claim, be more important to the discipline of literary criticism than to produce another interpretation of *King Lear*.
>
> But how is interpretation involved in a project like this? First, interpretations are part of the object of investigation. One would study plays, such as *King Lear*, which are reputed to involve catharsis, investigate what has been said about them, and discuss reactions with readers and viewers. One would be seeking to devise a theory to account for attested interpretations and reactions, not to produce a new interpretation of one's own. And note that the investigator's own reading of *Lear* is in principle irrelevant. He might judge Lear a silly old fool with no tragic grandeur in him, but he might still produce a compelling account of the mechanism of catharsis that accounted for the usual reactions to this and other plays. At this level, and this is the most important, interpretations are what the investigation studies, not what it seeks to produce.[2]

Note how the understanding of literature is divided from the experience of it. In producing "a compelling account of the mechanism of catharsis," the investigator has no obligation to experience catharsis. It would be difficult to imagine an experience of catharsis if Lear were thought to be a silly old fool.

The most effective challenge to structuralism and the

[2] *SCE* (Society for Critical Exchange) *Reports* 6 (Fall 1979), 79.

science of literature has come not from the old New Critics or traditional humanists, but from those who now carry the banner of advanced literary theory: most notably, the critics who call themselves deconstructionists. Much of what follows in this study concerns deconstruction in particular, but I want to pause here to say something about post-structuralist thinking in literary study, which is not confined to deconstruction. I have already spoken of the value placed on the individual work in the New Criticism. With the appearance of Northrop Frye and the structuralists interest shifts from the individual text to those features of a text that are commonly shared by other texts. The boundaries between individual texts are effectively erased. Nevertheless, what Frye and the structuralists have in common with the New Critics is a belief in the presence of texts. Texts are structures of worlds, plenitudes of meaning. These meanings can be interpreted and the conditions that generate them can be studied.

What characterizes post-structuralism is a questioning, indeed a denial of the independent or substantial existence of the text. Post-structuralist skeptics doubt or deny that the text in or of itself has presence. Thus Harold Bloom subscribes to this post-structuralist assumption, but with the regret of a disappointed believer in presence:

> The sad truth is that poems *don't have* presence, unity, form, or meaning. Presence is a faith, unity is a mistake or even a lie, form is a metaphor, and meaning is an arbitrary and now repetitious metaphysics. What then does a poem possess or create? Alas, a poem has nothing, and *creates* nothing.[3]

Paul de Man defines "true literary consciousness" (the consciousness of both writers and readers) as resulting not "from the absence of something but [from] the presence

[3] Harold Bloom, *Kabbalah and Criticism* (New York: The Seabury Press, 1975), p. 122

of a nothingness."[4] "Nothing," as Bloom and de Man conceive the term, has a metaphysical or theological resonance; in the case of Bloom we are sent to the Kabbalah,[5] in de Man to Nietzsche, Heidegger, and the continental philosophical tradition. In a reader-oriented critic like Stanley Fish, the intrinsic vacuity of the text is experienced as an empirical fact (though Fish is opposed to empiricism), devoid of metaphysical subtlety. For Fish the text is a series of marks on the page, which somehow have become estranged from the author who put them there. The marks do not in and of themselves constitute a structure or realize an intention; the text is realized only in the mind of the reader who is a member of an interpretive community that creates rather than discovers meaning. However different the versions, the authority of literary theory in post-structuralist criticism depends on the view that the text has no autonomous existence, that when we read a work we are in the presence of nothing.

Nothing, it should be said at once, is not to be confused with absence, as Hans-Georg Gadamer makes vividly clear in his objection to the following remark by Heidegger: "One cannot lose God as one loses his pocketknife."

[4] Quoted in Geoffrey Hartman, *Criticism in the Wilderness: The Study of Literature Today* (New Haven: Yale University Press, 1980), p. 179.

[5] In Kabbalah, Nothing is far from being the emptiness that it signifies in post-structuralist discourse. Indeed, it may be the most substantive of realities. "This *Nothing* from which everything has sprung is by no means a mere negation; only to us does it present no attributes because it is beyond the reach of intellectual knowledge. In truth, however, this Nothing—to quote one of the Kabbalists—is infinitely more real than all other reality. Only when the soul has stripped itself of all limitation and, in mystical language, has descended into the depths of Nothing does it encounter the Divine. For this *Nothing* comprises a wealth of mystical reality although it cannot be defined. 'Un Dieu defini serait un Dieu fini.' " Gershom G. Scholem, *Major Trends in Jewish Mysticism* (New York: Schocken Books, 1941), p. 25. In a work, Nothing signifies the divine itself, in its most impenetrable guise. And, in fact, *creation out of nothing* means to many mystics creation out of God.

> But in fact one cannot simply lose his pocketknife in such a fashion that it is no longer present. When one has lost a long familiar implement such as a knife, it demonstrates its existence by the fact that one continually misses it. Hölderlin's "Fehl der Götter" or Eliot's silence of the Chinese vase are [*sic*] not nonexistence, but "being" in the most poetic sense because they are silent. The breach that is made by what is missing is not a place remaining empty within what is present-to-hand; rather it belongs to the being-there of that to which it is missing, and is "present" in it.[6]

Absence implies presence, the opposite of nothingness.

That the text is an emptiness is hardly self-evident; in fact, it is plainly counterintuitive and opposed to common sense, as post-structuralist skeptics would be the first to admit. Indeed, the counterintuitive and uncommonsensical character of the view makes it a goad to literary theory. Every act of reading becomes a theoretical exercise which inconclusively demonstrates the presence of nothing against the untheoretical evidence of the senses.The exercise is made possible by a new demystifying sensitivity to the devious tropological nature of language, which is no longer seen as the evocative source of meaning and structure, but as an intrinsically deceptive medium of expression. Theoretical criticism, which becomes the only criticism worthy of the name, is a perpetual demystification of the illusion of fullness.

Deconstructive skepticism (the most radical and powerful of literary skepticisms) holds the view that the language of written discourse is inherently unreliable, that no matter how hard a text may try to sustain the illusion of unity, coherence, meaning, truth (attributes of presence and fullness), the text is incorrigibly prone to disunity, incoherence, meaninglessness, and error. For such skeptics, "reading"

[6] Hans-Georg Gadamer, *Philosophical Hermeneutics*, trans. David E. Linge (Berkeley and Los Angeles: University of California Press, 1976), p. 235.

becomes a deconstruction, a process of discovering the sources of error in a text. Indeed, the great texts (the deconstructive canon, so to speak) are those that know their own incoherence, in which case the critic is only a catalyst of the text's own deconstruction. Paul de Man need only touch a text of Rousseau and it deconstructs itself.

One may already remark as evidence of the unreliability of language a slippage in the use of the word "empty," which may now be understood as a structure of error. Such a structure, of course, is empty only in the Platonic sense, in which error is viewed as a privation or absence of substantial truth. In practice, of course, the encounter with a structure of error is experienced as an encounter with something—to be unraveled, deconstructed, demystified.

For those who have been brought up on the distinction (and separation) between beauty and truth, between poetry and philosophy, it is disconcerting to be confronted by a literary criticism inspired by the cognitive passion of philosophy. The poem, for example, is now denied the privilege of exempting itself from so-called rational discourse. Shelley's "Triumph of Life" or Yeats's "Among School Children" is subject to the same cognitive scrutiny as any other structure of discourse.

One misses the full force of deconstruction, however, if one ignores its anti-theological motive. As Murray Krieger remarks, the post-structuralist, if not structuralist impulse "may be seen as springing from the metaphysical (or rather anti-metaphysical) anguish that accompanies our sense of the 'disappearance of God.' "[7] Epistemologically, deconstructive skepticism is opposed to logocentric knowledge; theologically, to belief or faith. In contemporary literary discourse, knowledge is a version of "onto-theological" discourse. What is at stake in the skeptical challenge is the status both of our interpretive knowledge of texts and of

[7] Murray Krieger, *Poetic Presence and Illusion* (Baltimore: The Johns Hopkins University Press, 1979), p. 172.

our values and convictions. Unity, meaning, coherence, all targets of deconstructive suspicion, are tropes of both theology and epistemology. "The text is not a line of words [writes Roland Barthes in "The Death of the Author"] releasing a single 'theological' meaning (the 'message' of an Author-God) but a multidimensional space."[8] And elsewhere in the same essay, he asserts ". . . by refusing to assign a 'secret,' an ultimate meaning, to the text (and to the world as text), literature liberates what may be called an antitheological activity, an activity that is truly revolutionary since to refuse to fix meaning is, in the end, to refuse God and his hypostases—reason, science, law."[9] Deconstructive skepticism "puts in question" the god terms of humanist criticism. From a theological point of view, nothing is the nonpresence of God, the source and substance of being. All claims to presence in a text represent a view of literature as an expression of transcendence: the view, for example, that Matthew Arnold expresses in the opening paragraph of "The Study of Poetry."

> The future of poetry is immense, because in poetry, where it is worthy of its high destinies, our race, as time goes on, will find an ever surer and surer stay. There is not a creed which is not shaken, not an accredited dogma which is not shown to be questionable, not a received tradition which does not threaten to dissolve. Our religion has materialized itself in the fact, and now the fact is failing it. But for poetry the idea is everything; the rest is a world of illusion, of divine illusion. Poetry attaches its emotion to the idea; the idea *is* the fact. The strongest part of our religion today is its unconscious poetry.

My evocation of Arnold, of course, is not fortuitous, for Arnold gave to modern literary study its most powerful

[8] Roland Barthes, "The Death of the Author," in *Image-Music-Text*, trans. Stephen Heath (New York: Hill & Wang, 1977), p. 146

[9] Ibid., p. 147.

theology, a theology that still operates unconsciously in our belief in the power and value of literature.

The secular rationalist does not so much *believe* that the text is full, he takes it for granted, paradoxically because he is not burdened by religious expectations of plenitude and unity. He is content with the provisional unities and intelligibilities of the empirical world. What the comfortable objectivism of the secular rationalist fails to acknowledge (when he is comfortable in his empiricism) is that the truth of the objective world rests on the experience and reality of his own mind. When Descartes rediscovered the world through an act of radical doubt, he did not solve the problem of the subjective foundation of that world.

The confrontation between skeptical theory and humanist criticism, when it occurs, usually concerns questions of whether and how a text means and refers to the external world. Thus Gerald Graff argues forcefully and intelligently for mimetic realism against the post-structuralist view that discourse is the differential play of tropes, which may create only the illusion of reference.[10] Though I hold the view that there is an objective world and that it is represented in texts, I don't subscribe to the view that literature is essentially mimetic or that the mirror (the master image for mimesis) is a model for the imagination. Even the great realists of the nineteenth century (for example, George Eliot and Stendhal) implicitly admit the uncertain character of mimetic representation when they propose the defective or cracked mirror as an emblem of the novelist's imagination. It is an anomaly of realism that while it professes

[10] See Gerald Graff, *Literature Against Itself* (Chicago: University of Chicago Press, 1979). Graff does not subscribe to the mirror as a model for cognition. His allegiance is to Gombrich and Popper, who share with the romantics a belief in the priority of mind in the act of knowing, but for Graff, as for Gombrich and Popper, the product of imagination can and must be "matched" to the reality it represents. For Graff, the *telos* of imagination is realism; for the romantics, the *telos* of reality is its embodiment in imagination.

an historical view of the subject, the model that governs its own perception is *ahistorical* and passive. A mirror lacks a history, or to the extent that it does have a history that history diminishes its mirrorly qualities. Blemishes, cracks, darkenings distort the object as the mirror grows older. Or the mirror may be defective in its very construction. One does not need to subscribe to exalted claims for the imagination to acknowledge its active and transforming power. Novelists select, invent, and organize events.They do not photograph them, certainly not in the naive sense of photography. The critic has traditionally allowed the imaginative writer, even the so-called realistic novelist, imaginative rights, which have made challenges about the verisimilitude of novels seem impertinent and philistine. Critics do not expect novelists simply to mirror the world.

Yet traditionally critics have implicitly distinguished between the freedom of imagination and the responsibility of criticism. As interpreter and judge, the critic has been expected to demonstrate his objective faithfulness to the facts, let us say, of a novel. This distinction, however, has not been secure against demonstrations that the liveliest critics act upon, and don't merely reflect a text, which they may experience as a projection of their own desires and interests. One may hold a view of the imagination and intelligence as transforming or refractory faculties without denying an objective reality external to consciousness. In any event, the arguments for and against mimesis do not speak to the deconstructive critique of the transcendent source of the idea of reality or presence in the text.

Deconstructive or anti-theological skepticism does not exhaust the possibilities of skepticism, which can also be a negative capability, the productive source of freedom and plenitude. I will have something to say about this version of skepticism in Chapter 7. The skeptic disposition, however, with which I am principally concerned is of the anti-theological dogmatic variety, which dominates literary study today. I speak of a *disposition* in order to suggest that what is at stake is not merely a matter of cognition. The conviction of certainty or of uncertainty is rarely the conclusion of an argument, however rigorous its logic; it is rather the result of a temperamental or willful need to see text and world in a certain way. Doubt or certitude, the conviction of emptiness or fullness, are anterior to logic and evidence.

It is not sheer disinterestedness that leads me to this study. The desacralizing anti-theological motive of contemporary skepticism creates an opportunity for an antithetical speculation. One has no choice but to admit the problematic subjectivity of our knowledge of the world and of texts, a subjectivity whose divine origins are by no means certain. This much at least has to be conceded to the deconstructive critique. It does not follow, however, from the problematic character of our subjectivity that we must abandon it to the corrosive acid of dogmatic skepticism.

Deconstructive skepticism is simultaneously directed toward the subject and the object. It does not privilege one above the other. If it does not evaporate either term, it is not from want of trying. Most of the defense against deconstructive skepticism has been conducted on behalf of the object. What has been insufficiently remarked is that the disappearance of the (transcendental) subject would entail the loss of our value-making power, which is the secular meaning of transcendence. Evaluation has been a peripheral, if not discredited, activity in literary study for a considerable time, the consequence of an unreflective positivism. Since an evaluation of a work cannot be objectively verified, it can only be regarded as an expression of a subjectivity, which by definition is unreliable. Having inherited the professional mistrust of evaluation as a subjective activity, post-structuralist criticism has extended the mistrust to interpretation itself. Evaluation at its best is a complex and structured activity of the mind, which discriminates for use (here broadly conceived) the objects of the world. Evaluation necessarily expresses the needs and interests of the evaluator. Without conceding that he hallucinates the facts, the evaluative critic may acknowledge without compromising his activity that he doesn't simply mirror the object since desiring, needing, even judging are inevitably refractory. Without evaluation the objects of the world would engulf each one of us. What follows is neither an argument for subjectivism or objectivism, but rather an effort to respond to the legitimate and rational claims of both the subject and the object in their various conditions of continuity with and estrangement from one another.

I begin with the legacy of Matthew Arnold, who in his own time sought to arrest the desacralization of literature by a saving relocation of its transcendental claims from heaven to earth.

1

CRITICISM AT THE PRESENT TIME

In a review of the Rockefeller Foundation report on *The Humanities in American Life,* Hilton Kramer remarks that "we are a long way here from Matthew Arnold's notion of trying 'to know the best that is known and thought in the world.' " And he ruefully observes that "Arnold's name . . . is never mentioned in this report, which so systematically avoids any mention of our classic writers that one is left wondering what this committee has in mind when it speaks of the humanities."[1] Once the inspiration of humanistic study in England and America, Arnold has now become something of an embarrassment. He represents for many an abandoned path or a path to be abandoned.

Arnold has had a complex fate in contemporary literary discussion. His direct influence on the study of literature has been minimal since the advent of the New Criticism. For all their astuteness and penetration, Arnold's remarks about literature were too casual, too remote from the text to nourish a criticism devoted to close and systematic observation of individual works. Though the New Critics also had views of society and history, and though they were willing when necessary to use historical information to explicate texts, they tended to separate the aesthetic character of the work from its historical and social implications.

Arnold's presence in contemporary literary discussion is often expressed through the terms "history" and "society."

[1] *New York Times Book Review,* Dec. 28, 1980, p. 1.

To speak of Arnold's presence in the work of contemporary critics is not to imply agreement in judgment (whether aesthetic or political or social) between him and his epigoni. Raymond Williams, for example, is an acute critic of the conservative tendency in Arnold's thought. The affinity between them is one of perspective, of discipline, of concern with subject matter. Lionel Trilling acknowledged the superiority of the New Critics to Arnold in the close attention they give to texts, but he preferred to see literature as a social and historical activity. His work has a speculative range that transcends the boundaries implied by New Critical doctrine.[2]

But the interest in society and history does not fully express Arnold's abiding presence in literary studies. In 1940 Trilling spoke of Arnold as having "shaped the academic opinions" of our time and as having "established the teaching of English literature as an academic profession."[3] The legacy of Arnold is, in T. S. Eliot's phrase, "the common pursuit of judgment and the correction of taste." No one pursued judgment and taste more passionately than F. R. Leavis, who more than any other modern critic defined the *moral* discipline of the academic study of literature. With his Hellenistic sensitivity to the excesses of Hebraistic passion, Arnold might have recoiled from the Puritan fervors of Leavis, but he would have acknowledged a shared sense of mission to formulate and uphold literary standards and to foster the vitality of language against the prevailing philistinism of the majority culture. Even modern writers like

[2] Note I say doctrine rather than practice, because any close attention to New Critical practice will discover latitudes and transgressions hardly in keeping with doctrinaire attitudes. Moreover, when one considers the variety of doctrine that goes under the name New Criticism, one hesitates to deny speculative range to particular New Critics. Blackmur, Burke (is he a New Critic?), Ransom, Tate: they do not restrict themselves to close reading, but there is nevertheless an ideological disposition to rein in speculation that does not serve to illuminate the particular text. In this respect, Burke is not a New Critic.

[3] "Literature and Power," *Kenyon Review* 2 (Autumn 1940), 96.

Eliot and Ezra Pound, who rejected Arnold's touchstones for modern literature, subscribed to the anti-philistine creed that he had articulated.

There are few critics at the present time dedicated to this social purpose. Now and then one hears a voice lamenting the decline of standards and the abuse of language, but whatever the merit of the criticism, the voice sounds cranky and impertinent to professional writers and teachers of English. In America at least, the voice of Culture provokes a populist resentment which has intensified since the advent of the counterculture in the Sixties. Professional linguists reinforce the resentment by stressing the richness of local or ethnic dialects, which the high cultural view represses. In this perspective Culture with a capital *C* is perceived as a parochialism. Arnold's tone is often embarrassing to modern ears. "Arnold's high-minded defense of culture," Gerhard Joseph remarks in a recent essay on Arnold, "seems both overly pious and palpable [*sic*] in an age that prefers the nonpedagogical virtues of understatement and indirection."[4] The impersonality of the observation distances Joseph in a thoroughly modern fashion from a commitment to the defense of Culture. Piety here is not a matter of substance, but of style, and the style is an embarrassment to the modern sensibility. The pedagogues of culture are wary of pedagogical virtues. For Harold Bloom, for example, the social, cultural, and literary critic (not to say distinguished poet) Arnold has been reduced to one of his roles, pedagogue to the uninitiated, in Bloom's phrase, "the greatest of all School Inspectors."[5]

In his essay "The Two Environments: Reflections on the Study of English" (1965), Lionel Trilling asked "whether in our culture the study of literature is any longer a suitable

[4] "The Antigone as Cultural Touchstone: Matthew Arnold, Hegel, George Eliot, Virginia Woolf and Margaret Drabble," *PMLA* 96 (Jan. 1981), 29.

[5] "The Breaking of Form," in *Deconstruction and Criticism*, ed. Harold Bloom, Paul de Man, Jacques Derrida, Geoffrey Hartman, and J. Hillis Miller (New York: The Seabury Press, 1979), p. 7.

means for developing and refining the intelligence."[6] Trilling's question is addressed to the substance of literary culture as well as to its style and tone. Trilling's Arnoldian credentials give the question an unsettling authority. In his last years, Trilling became an elegist of a view that he had long cherished. The erosion of literary culture as a social idea has been a long and continuous process since Arnold's time.

For Matthew Arnold in the 1860s, literary culture had occupied a critical position vis-à-vis the twin evils of Jacobinism and philistinism: that is, the left and right of the middle-class revolution that England and France had both experienced, though in different ways. Jacobinism was the principle and energy that had created the revolution, and philistinism was the complacent life that had installed itself as a consequence of it. From a political point of view, philistinism is the betrayal of Jacobin principle, the conservative outcome of the revolution. But literary culture, in Arnold's work, made it possible to perceive an ethos common to both Jacobinism and philistinism. It was an ethos characterized by narrowness and bigotry, fanatical in its commitment to certain political ideas (in the case of Jacobinism) and certain religious and economic ideas (in the case of philistinism). Nobility, sincerity, simplicity, disinterestedness—all the value terms of Culture—Arnold found securely embedded in a literary tradition that had remained attached to the highest ideals of Christianity. Though Arnold was an acute witness of a process of secularization that would eventually sever literature from those religious ideals, he wrote at a time when secularization meant an eliciting rather than a demystifying of the values to be found both in secular literature and in the scriptures. For Arnold, literary culture reveals the hidden meaning of Christianity.

In *Literature and Dogma* (a work that had enormous contemporary appeal), Arnold insists on St. Paul's *literary* use

[6] In *Beyond Culture* (New York: Viking Press, 1968), p. 232.

of terms like "grace," "new birth," and "justification," which, in Arnold's view, have been "blunderingly taken in a fixed and rigid manner, as if they were symbols with as definite and fully grasped a meaning as the names *line* or *angle*." Paul's language must be read as metaphors for inner states of feeling. Reciprocally, it requires a kind of religious sensitivity to perceive the spiritual character of poetry. "The Study of Poetry" (1880) begins with the passage I have already quoted in the Introduction in which Arnold charts a religious destiny for poetry. It is difficult to define the precise character of Arnold's religious convictions. Though he lacked a mystical sensibility and probably mistrusted all accounts of the supernatural as evidence of a dogmatizing intellect, he had a profound feeling for the transcendental character of the religious idea, of what he called the "power not ourselves which makes for righteousness."

It is this transcendental space that culture comes to occupy, to the enormous advantage of Arnold as a literary and social critic. Thus in *Culture and Anarchy*, the cultural critic writing from the elevation and conviction of perfection, can reveal the partiality, the distortions, and the limitations of class behavior. His voice is reasonable and balanced. If there is a vice toward which it tends, it is smug self-congratulation. To our modern ears, it may sound excessively pious. When the conviction persists after literature has been cut off from its transcendental moorings (as in the case of Leavis), there may be a compensation in passion: a sense of outraged incredulity at the general insensitivity to the light.

It is revealing of the modern response to Arnold that Leavis in his generally appreciative *Scrutiny* essay on "Arnold as Critic" (1938) would speak of the opening of "The Study of Poetry" as representing the "element that 'dates' Arnold's work in the worst sense."[7] Leavis does not like the

[7] *A Selection from Scrutiny*, comp. F. R. Leavis, 2 vols. (Cambridge: Cambridge University Press, 1968), 1:261.

explicitness with which Arnold attaches poetry to a religious destiny (or conversely, religion to a poetic destiny). But it is significant that he does not disavow the relationship between religion and poetry. Though he criticizes the "unqualified intention of the passage," wonders about Arnold's qualifications as a theologian and philosopher, and refers with sympathy to "the many who deplore Arnold's way with religion," he speaks in Arnoldian fashion of the importance of preserving the literary tradition in the wake of the relaxation of other traditions and social forms. It is not clear from Leavis's account how Arnold might have done his job better. Leavis's objection may rest simply on his preference for a strenuous evasion of certain kinds of explicitness, which always suggest to him alien intrusions of systematic philosophy and science into literary discourse. And indeed, what Leavis values in Arnold is Arnold's dislike of system, or what Leavis calls "inappropriate criteria of logical rigor and 'definition.' " In short, Arnold for Leavis is a *literary* critic with extraordinary judgment and tact, who in his best work knew how and where to point in a poem to reveal its distinction or its weakness. In writing in defense of the "touchstone" (not of Arnold's particular touchstones) Leavis justifies his own method. "It is a tip for mobilizing our sensibility; for focusing our relevant experience in a sensitive point; for reminding us vividly of what the best is like."[8] Leavis is, of course, right to stress Arnold's literary character without which theological speculation about literature is sterile. But Arnold's authority does not derive simply from Arnold's power of literary discrimination. Leavis's evasiveness about Arnold's religious interests does not help us in understanding that authority.

In *Matthew Arnold and American Culture* John Raleigh divides Arnold's modern influence between Eliot and Trilling in a misleading way. "If Eliot took the poetic-religious side of Arnold for his starting point,Trilling has appropriated

[8] Ibid., p. 265.

the socio-liberal side."[9] It is true that Eliot quarreled with what he understood to be Arnold's confusion. ("The total effect of Arnold's philosophy," Eliot observes in his essay on Arnold and Pater, "is to set up Culture in the place of Religion and to leave Religion to be laid waste by the anarchy of feelings.") It is also true that Trilling seems both to avoid the religious theme in Arnold's work and to be critical of Eliot's religious dogmatism. ("I consider it from many points of view an impropriety to try to guarantee literature by religious belief.") But the virtues that Trilling espouses have their source in the religious idea. Intelligence, disinterestedness, courage, modulation, and flexibility may have lost their religious sanction in Trilling's advocacy, but they can be traced back to Arnold's "literary" reading of the Bible. Trilling's career-long struggle with the imperial will in its various guises (politics, art, intellect, instinct) has a "religious" resonance. It is as if Trilling had perceived an overweening pride in the various efforts to deny the conditioned character of existence.

The appeals to sensibility in both Trilling and Leavis have a moral (rather than an exclusively aesthetic) force that can best be understood as a residuum of an originally religious inspiration. When Trilling endorses Leavis's preferences for Dr. Johnson and Arnold over Coleridge, he characterizes those preferences as ones in which the critic requires "no first principles for his judgment but only the sensibility that is the whole response of his whole being."[10] For the *whole* (the essential word here) not to be vacuous, it must contain a strong trace of the spiritual experience that Arnold insisted upon. Similarly, "society" and "community" are value terms, not simply empirical constructions: they carry within them the religious idea.

For Arnold, literary and social interests are intimately

[9] *Matthew Arnold and American Culture* (Berkeley and Los Angeles: University of California Press, 1957), p. 220.

[10] Ibid., p. 234.

related to one another because the process of secularization discloses the religious function of both literary and social life.[11] Society is the arena in which the best self is realized. Arnold's disturbing exaltation of the State proceeds from an idealized conflation of social and political categories. It was still possible in Arnold's time to conceive of society as a possible space for spiritual fulfillment, despite the quite different character of actual society. Criticism thrived on the difference between ideal and actual society.The social critic of the nineteenth century (Coleridge, Carlyle, Ruskin, Arnold, Morris) had available to him pasts (not yet demystified) that provided models of spiritual (organic) community. These pasts were derived from literature, not from actual political and social history, and were thus protected as models from the brute facts of the past. For Coleridge, Carlyle, Ruskin, or Morris the past was medieval, for Arnold Hellenistic.

The confidence that sustains the social criticism of the nineteenth century disappears in the wake of the increasing bureaucratic rationalization of modern society. It becomes difficult if not impossible to think of society as a place of possible fulfillment. The process of secularization no longer elicits the spiritual truths of social life; it undermines them. What occurs (as in the case of Eliot) is a critique of the secular humanistic habit of regarding social life as an autonomous source of spiritual value. And the critique is conducted in behalf of religious orthodoxy, which itself seems hardly possible in the modern world. The consequence is an enfeeblement of social criticism.[12]

Literature as anything but a corpus of individual works assumes an ideological affiliation. To speak of literature is

[11] See Emile Durkheim's *The Elementary Forms of the Religious Life* for a sustained and complex definition of society as the hidden object of religious worship.

[12] See the chapter on Eliot, "The Reality of Disillusion in T. S. Eliot" in my book *The Failure of Criticism* (Cambridge, Mass.: Harvard University Press, 1978).

to have a particular idea of it as a collective activity. When Arnold characterizes the power of literature as that of enabling us to see life whole, he conceives of literature as an enlargement of the religious idea. As he himself acknowledged, he was continuing the work of his father Thomas Arnold. He writes to his mother:

> But something of what Papa did as against the Evangelicals—an enlarging of the idea of religion—is the great want of our spiritual and intellectual life of England at present. . . . Papa's greatness consists in his bringing such a torrent of freshness in English religion, by placing history and politics in connexion with it.[13]

In contemporary discussion of Arnold (whatever of it exists), the religious theme is usually overlooked as a source of his literary and social interests. The decline of religious authority in the modern period does not reduce literature to individual works. Rather, literature acquires new identities. In its radical modernist form, it develops a partiality and combativeness, what Trilling was to call its adversary character. No longer standing above the fray in disinterested contemplation of the benighted passions of other participants in the cultural and political arena, literature becomes aggressive in its own interests. Wanting ascendancy in whatever it affirms or denigrates, literature is no longer embarrassed to reveal its will to power. In its academic form literature becomes literary study. In the interests of professionalism literary scholars maintain the "integrity" of their subject by resisting any usurpation of it that might introduce impurities: the confusion of genres, the subordination of the "scientific" or "literary" character of literary study to religious or political interests. Literature is not to be confused with other academic departments: philosophy, theology, history, sociology, and so on.

[13] Letter dated "Thursday Morning," Nov. 18, 1865, cited by Sidney Coulling, *Matthew Arnold and His Critics* (Athens: Ohio University Press, 1974), p. 193.

It may be objected that literature is not sufficiently monolithic to be defined by a single act. But generalizations about literature that do not encompass all its variety are inevitable and even necessary. By identifying literature with one of its tendencies, the generalization (or its maker) means to privilege that tendency, to make it dominant. It is not mere arbitrariness that channels the literary imagination in a certain direction, but an intuition shared by creative writers and critics that for the moment the most potent and interesting energies of the imagination want to unfold in a particular direction. There is, of course, always the risk of repressing other energies, especially when the privileged energies have spent themselves or perhaps were never genuine in the first place and are sustained by the arbitrariness of fashion. There is also the risk of confusing the historical career of literature or a particular moment in that career with universal, timeless theoretical statements about the nature of literature. We must always remind ourselves that all theories, however universalist they seem, are, as Geoffrey Hartman has remarked, canon-specific. They belong to, but do not encompass, the history of literature. But without these privileging generalizations, literature has no historical career.

Cut off from religion, literature becomes a thing of the world like an object of scientific study, devoid of essential mystery. Attributions of unfathomable mystery are little more than mystifications, vestiges of what Geoffrey Hartman calls "lost-object" theorizing. In this perspective, "true literary consciousness," as Paul de Man observes, "never results from the absence of something but consists of the presence of a nothingness." Literary theory and criticism has or should have as its motive the undoing (deconstruction) of all literary pretensions to depth, transcendence, interiority; all the terms that denote presence. This is not to say that a work of literature may ever be exhaustively known. Some corner of the work may remain in darkness, but the darkness is not intrinsic to the work; it is rather a function of the mind's incorrigible will to delusion, since the mind cannot tolerate a sustained look into the abyss.

As a philosophical movement, deconstruction can be viewed as an attempt to complete the process of desacralization of literature that Arnold tried to arrest. But deconstruction itself enounters resistance in its own knowledge of the mind's resistance to the "truth" of "nothingness." Thus literature remains in a residual or instinctive way even for the most "sophisticated" minds a compensation for a lost presence, an emanation or trace of the transcendent mystery from which we are estranged. Literary discussion persists in assuming the palpable existence of unfathomable mystery. I speak of this view half-consciously or unconsciously held because its implications are rarely faced. If they were faced, very few reader-critics would be willing to accept them. I suspect that most would prefer the conscious inconsistency of denying to literature its transcendental pretensions while using the language of transcendence in appreciations of literature. Arnold belongs to our residual instinctive feeling for literature, but he is an embarrassment to our understanding of it. This division of feeling is reflected in the deconstructionist's insistence that there is an insurmountable gulf between literary understanding (theory) and experience, and his preference for understanding at the expense of experience. Theory keeps one at a skeptical distance from the always "naive" experience of literature.

Any account of what informs the continuing interest in literature of some of our most influential critics would have to include the pleasure in the experience of the skeptical intelligence against the spiritual claims of literature. It is true that a residual conviction remains about the beauty and importance of literature, but an articulation of the conviction inevitably encounters irony. Since "value" and "significance" are terms one finds in "naive" talk about literature, those who wish to resist current standards of sophistication without appearing naive frequently divert discussion to questions about the intelligibility and referentiality of texts.

For Arnold the task of criticism was to see "the object as it in itself it really is," implying the objective intelligibility of the work. Arnold derived the formula from Wordsworth's attribution of visionary power to the poet. The object for both Wordsworth and Arnold was not a mere thing of the world, it was a transparency for transcendental meaning or value. The literary apprehension of the work (whether poetic or critical) rivaled what was understood to be a scientific view. Contemporary discussions about objective intelligibility and referentiality solicit our scientific or philosophical curiosity. "Intelligibility" and "referentiality" become substitutes for the kind of conviction or engagement that Arnold represents.[14]

The devaluation of literary experience in modern critical theory (particularly in its deconstructionist version) is of no small consequence to what I have characterized as the social purpose of literature and literary study. For it is our moral as well as aesthetic experience of both language and literature that determines our valuing truth, lucidity, precision, and elegance. If that experience is dismissed as naive and unworthy of serious understanding, aesthetic and moral discriminations about the uses of language and the quality of imagination become a matter of whim and "mere" taste. There is no *necessary* force, for example, in the ironies Arnold directs at the philistine or those that George Orwell directs at the pretensions of intellectuals, for the values that

[14] In *Literature Against Itself* (Chicago: University of Chicago Press, 1979) Gerald Graff argues with the passion of a social critic against those who deny the propositional sense of literature and its power to represent reality, and he is illuminating, though too sweeping, in his judgment of the motives for certain nonrepresentational views. But Graff does not show how the experience of literature or the kind of conviction that animates his book is nourished by a belief in the propositional sense of literature and its representational power.

empower those ironies are themselves subject to a deconstructive understanding. To be sure, deconstructionists aspire to rigor in their analyses, but it is characteristic of that rigor that any stabilizing term that can provide a basis for assured judgment is suspect.

The desacralization of literature eventually dissolves the basis for a literary-inspired criticism that distinguishes, for example, between honest and deceitful uses of language or between enlightened and barbarous cultural institutions. I don't mean that one has to hold Arnold's specific view of the relations between Christianity and literature to be a judicial literary and social critic, but one has to have some kind of belief in values that inhere in literary experience, and those values have their source in religious thought. Even Northrop Frye, who tries to turn literary study into a science, knows this, and this knowledge works against his scientific project.[15]

Much has been made of Arnold's vagueness as a religious thinker and of his unfortunate confounding of religion with literature. What must be remembered is that the perspective from which Arnold has been judged to be inept and confused is that of Christian orthodoxy. Eliot's strictures about Arnold's theology are in a sense a reenactment of early Christian castigations of the Gnostic heresy, which rejected the literalist understanding of Christ's passion and resurrection and insisted upon the symbolic character of the career of Jesus. The view of the Bible as literature, the privileging of poetry as the vehicle of spiritual experience,

[15] As I wrote in *The Failure of Criticism*: "For all his modernist skepticism, Frye does not want to give up the humanist ideal altogether. Though Frye disparages views of culture that have a definite image of a future and perhaps attainable society, for its tendency to purge the tradition, he endorses the Arnoldian version of culture 'which seeks to do away with classes.' In Frye's view, neither the present nor the future contains the possibility of such a society, but culture or the imagination is the place where such a society can be 'realized' and enjoyed. 'The imaginative element of works of art . . . lifts them clear of the bondage of history' " (p. 19).

the habit of viewing god terms as emblems of spiritual, psychological, and moral states, the identification of the knowledge of God with self-knowledge, the rationalistic bias in the understanding of scriptures: these are elements in the Gnostic heresy that one rediscovers in the higher criticism of the nineteenth century.

For Arnold, as for the Gnostics, man is the source of value, which he embodies in a condition of otherness so as to absolutize and stabilize value. In *The Gnostic Gospels*, Elaine Pagels notes that "the gnostic Valentinus taught that humanity itself manifests the divine life and divine revelation. The church, he says, consists of that portion of humanity that recognizes and celebrates its divine origins."[16] From the orthodox point of view, there is the danger that Man becomes men, the effect of which would be to destabilize and relativize values, which in turn can become disguises for personal interests. Here the orthodox critic would be addressing himself to what he considers to be the implications of consequences of a doctrine, not its intention. Arnold's intention is to realize the value-making capacity of religion.

The major critics of the nineteenth century (Carlyle and Ruskin as well as Arnold) equivocated between a desire to retain the traditional religious vocabulary and an effort to discover a new language appropriate to the extraordinary changes occuring in modern life. (In *Sartor Resartus* Carlyle acknowledges that the "authentic Church-Catechism of our present century has not yet fallen into my hands: meanwhile, for my private behoof, I attempt to elucidate the matter so." The elucidation requires that he use the language of Christianity in a metaphorical or psychological sense.) What remains firm, though not undisturbed, is a commitment to spiritual truth as it had been defined by the Christian tradition.

It is an unquestionable power of the deconstructive at-

[16] *The Gnostic Gospels* (New York: Random House, 1979), p. 147.

titude that it does not temporize with the religious aspirations of literary consciousness. The rigorous consistency with which it deconstructs all such aspirations forces our closet religiosities and humanisms out into the open. In accomplishing their feat, deconstructionists have not demonstrated the "nothingness" that they say is present everywhere, but they require us to do what no one has yet adequately done: to rearticulate the absent something that we continue to experience.

When we try to rearticulate the kind of humanism that Arnold represents, we have an immediate sense of its inadequacy for our time. How does a literary-inspired social criticism confront an enormity like the Holocaust? Whether we think of the whole man in its Arnoldian Hebraistic-Hellenistic variant or in some other variant, the terms of humanism seem pitifully inadequate to the event. Even lesser enormities (and our century is replete with examples) seem to call for the kind of understanding unavailable to humanism.[17]

But one is putting excessive pressure on humanism by invoking the enormity of the Holocaust. To say that humanism is inadequate to the Holocaust is not to invalidate

[17] As Saul Bellow has remarked:

> The Holocaust may be seen as a deliberate lesson or project in philosophical redefinition: "You religious and enlightened people, you Christians, Jews and Humanists, you believers in freedom, dignity and enlightenment—you think you know what a human being is. Look at our camps and crematoria, and see if you can bring your hearts to care about these millions."
>
> And it is obvious that the humanistic civilized moral imagination is inadequate. Confronted with such a "metaphysical" demonstration, it despairs and declines from despair into lethargy and sleep.

To Jerusalem and Back (New York: Viking Press, 1976), p. 58. Yet the humanistic imagination continues to be heard in the voice of Bellow, even here in the passage I have just quoted. Imagine what it would be like if it were extinguished or forgotten. Moreover, as contemporary literature has testified, no response to the horrors of the modern period has been adequate.

it for our daily lives; it is rather to circumscribe its imaginative and moral power. No response is adequate to the Holocaust, but no response *at all* is even less adequate. Humanism did not produce the Holocaust, and the Holocaust, knowing its enemies, was bent on the extermination of humanism. It is an odd consequence of an all-or-nothing mentality to repudiate humanist values because they are inadequate as an antidote to an evil.

We do need to rethink the meaning of the emblematic presence of Arnold in literary study, as Trilling and Williams have done, each in his own way. Arnold is not simply a collection of particular judgments with which we might strongly disagree (e.g., that Chaucer lacks high seriousness as a writer, that the romantics were deficient in ideas, that strikes are dangerous to the social order, that the State should be the authoritative agent of Culture, and so on). He represents a kind of attention toward literature, culture, and society the content of which needs to be reimagined with every historical change. To reimagine the content of criticism is to avoid a sterile classicism and to provide a genuine alternative to the innovations of advanced criticism. What remains constant is some version of the religious idea about literature as a living expression of men and women. The crux of the matter is the very idea of transcendence.

Arnold himself understood that the transcendental space was "a very small circle." Its aim was to generate the values and convictions (touchstones, in Arnold's metaphor) from which perspective the triumphant movements that pass upon the stage of history are to be criticized. Those who work within the circle do not hope to constitute a triumphant movement (they even cherish their attachments to defeated causes), but the criticism always tells upon the mind, saps the "adversaries' positions" and keeps up its "communications with the future" (*Culture and Anarchy*). The critics cannot hope to constitute a triumphant movement, because all such movements suffer rigidity and corruption, the indignities of success in the world. If the critics remain attached to defeated causes, it is not because of a retrograde nostalgia for the past, but because of their commitment to the idea or ideal that survives the defeat, an ideal that *transcends* the vicissitudes of its action in history. What makes the small circle a "transcendent space" makes it the place from which one can't achieve ascendancy in the world.

Paradoxically, transcendence is now an immanent presence in the world. Is it possible that the vulnerability of transcendence to demystification and deconstruction derives from the literalness with which the metaphor is read? Transcendence locates the source of values beyond the world, whereas now it is to be located within the world—that is, within a communally defined human faculty. One wants to preserve the term transcendence, because the term suggests the necessary distinction between the actual and the unrealized (the ground of criticism).

It is, of course, true that bringing transcendence down to earth and locating it within the human mind disturbs the security and stability it enjoys in its divine setting. The implications of permanence and stability in Arnold's formulations misrepresent the new location of transcendence. But it doesn't necessarily follow from its new location that "the transcendental space" is a mystification, a naiveté, a futile stay against the corrosions of time. The incorrigible persistence of what the deconstructive skeptics call mystification and naiveté has its source in the inextinguishable human need for values and the assent to values that we call conviction.[18] In trying "to put in question" (a favorite locution of deconstructive skepticism) the onto-theological status of every production of values, the deconstructive skeptics in effect subvert the very activity of value-making.

[18] See Arnold's "The Function of Criticism at the Present Time." My defense of transcendence was inspired by Stuart Tave's critical response to an earlier version of this chapter in *Critical Inquiry* 9 (Mar. 1983).

Oddly enough, Geoffrey Hartman's recent critique of Arnold in *Criticism in the Wilderness* displaces its focus from the transcendental space, which Hartman recognizes, to what he calls the Arnoldian Concordat: the "agreement" that Arnold effected between creativity and criticism. Hartman deplores the concordat because 1) it assumes a radical distinction between criticism and creativity, and 2) it arranges a peace between the activities so conceived at the expense of the creative energies of criticism. The passage in "The Function of Criticism" from which Hartman draws the title of his book presents the inferiority of criticism in the figure of the precursor.

> There is the promised land toward which criticism can only beckon. That promised land will not be ours to enter, and we shall die in the wilderness; but to have desired to enter it, to have saluted it from afar, is already the best distinction among contemporaries.

It should be said immediately in response to Hartman's charge that though Arnold does indeed speak of the inferiority of criticism to creativity, the program that he actually establishes for criticism in a sense belies the distinction that he makes, and that is the basis of Hartman's discontent with him. Arnold understands criticism to be a speculative function that generates an atmosphere of ideas in which imaginative literature can prosper. Though not abstract and systematic like philosophy, criticism is in practice a creative activity. Arnold chooses not to call it creative, because he wants to privilege poetic imagination with that term. His poetical bias misleads him and his readers about the creative character of criticism and of his own criticism.[19]

[19] Murray Krieger suggests that "it may well be argued that Arnold is invoking these distinctions—and arguing for the primacy, indeed the greater creativity, of the critical rather than the creative—in order to justify, to himself as to others, his own decision to turn his career from poetry to criticism." *Poetic Presence and Illusion* (Baltimore: The Johns Hopkins University Press, 1979), p. 94.

For Arnold criticism as a speculative function is not a dependent activity. On the contrary, it is imaginative literature that depends on the prior activity of criticism for its full success. Here is the crucial passage from "The Function of Criticism":

> It is the business of the critical power . . . "in all branches of knowledge, theology, philosophy, history, art, science, to see the object as in itself it really is!" Thus it tends, at last, to make an intellectual situation of which the creative power can profitably avail itself. It tends to establish an order of ideas, if not absolutely true, yet true by comparison with that which it displaces; to make the best ideas prevail. Presently these new ideas reach society, the touch of truth is the touch of life, and there is a stir and growth everywhere; out of this stir and growth come the creative epochs of literature.

The failure of romantic poetry, according to Arnold, is in the fact that it has been insufficiently nourished by the work of "the critical power." Hartman, of course, acknowledges this passage, but he denies the *creative* function of criticism in Arnold when he speaks deflatingly of its role as merely "circulating" or even "stimulating" ideas. Arnold does not help matters by being obscure about how much invention is involved in making the order of ideas prevail.

Arnold's biblical rhetoric, if not his distinction-making, suggests the prophetic character of the critic. In his plea for creative criticism, Hartman recalls the elevation and power that Arnold grants to the critic.

> Arnold identifies the critics, of whom he is one, with the generation that was destined to perish in the Sinai desert. But this wilderness is all we have. Arnold's fiction of presence was that our errand in the wilderness would end: that a new and vital literature would arise to redeem the work of the critic. What if this literature is not unlike criticism, and we are forerunners to ourselves? Perhaps

> it is better that the wilderness should be the Promised Land, than vice-versa.[20]

Here at least Hartman and Arnold are on the same terrain. The enormous appeal of *Criticism in the Wilderness* is that for all its post-structuralist sophistication, it retains an undeconstructed desire for a creative critical activity beyond skepticism.

The displacement of focus, I would suggest, results from an unacknowledged desire in Hartman to reserve some of that transcendent energy for his conception of criticism. Since the transcendental dispensation is no longer available to him (Hartman follows deconstruction here) he can try to recover it (without acknowledging its source) in the idea of creativity. In a review of *Criticism in the Wilderness*, I distinguish Hartman from a deconstructive skeptic like Derrida in the following way: ". . . Hartman's irrepressible playfulness . . . remains faithful to the pathos of the romantic inspiration; the world is full for him, not empty as it is for Derrida."[21] What creative critical activity amounts to when it is devoid of pathos is a play of tropes always in danger of becoming, in Hartman's own words, "leprously insubstantial."[22]

Toward the end of *Criticism in the Wilderness*, Hartman addresses himself to the question of the role of criticism in a society whose ambition is the higher education of the masses. It is the kind of question that can be addressed from a perspective one finds in Arnold's work. And Hartman is squarely within that perspective when he proposes a combined English-business major as a way of humanizing our business culture. What is not given to Hartman or to any of his contemporaries is the social imagination of the nineteenth century. Consider the wealth of invention, wit,

[20] Hartman, *Criticism in the Wilderness* (New Haven: Yale University Press, 1980), p. 15.

[21] See "The Creativity of Criticism," *ADE Bulletin* 67 (Spring 1981), 39.

[22] Hartman, *Criticism in the Wilderness*, p. 179.

irony, and moral power in *Culture and Anarchy*. Hellenism and Hebraism, barbarians and philistines are key metaphors in a series of elaborate conceits that body forth a whole society. Arnold wrote in what was already a nineteenth-century prophetic tradition including Carlyle, Ruskin, Emerson, and Thoreau. To say that the social imagination is not given to Hartman is to speak of a condition of the times, not of a personal limitation in him. Indeed, one must be grateful to Hartman for the way he compels the question of the power and significance of criticism to emerge from the experience of post-structuralist criticism.

The source of power in Arnold was an indivisible transcendental space, which made his apostolic view of culture possible.

> The great men of culture are those who have had a passion for diffusing, for making prevail, for carrying from one end of society to the other, the best knowledge, the best ideas of their time; who have laboured to divest knowledge of all that was harsh, uncouth, difficult, abstract, professional, exclusive; to humanize it, to make it efficient outside the clique of the cultivated and the learned yet remaining the *best* knowledge and thought of the time . . .

It is ironic that the deconstructionists have to remind us what the source of power in Arnold *was*, even if we have become too "sophisticated" to repossess it.

It is true, as Hartman notes, that Arnold was profoundly critical of the "French mania" for translating ideas into political imperatives or ideologies. (The "grand error of the French Revolution," Arnold observes in "The Function of Criticism at the Present Time" was that "by quitting the intellectual sphere and rushing furiously into the political sphere" it "produced no such intellectual fruit as the movement of ideas of the Renascence.") Arnold opposed the critical faculty, which has in his version of it a distinctly English positivist cast, to the paradoxically abstract and prematurely practical bent of the French. However mistrustful he was of abstraction and system, Arnold was nevertheless by native standards one of the few speculative critics in the English tradition. By drawing a circle around Arnold and the New Critics and making them his targets, Hartman implicitly holds Arnold responsible for what is really a strong critical reaction against him. The conflation of Arnold and the New Criticism gives a misleading impression of the ways in which both Arnold and the New Critics differ from contemporary literary speculation.

While contemporary literary theory continues to sanction an interest in the close "reading" of texts, which the New Criticism had installed, that reading is in the service of philosophical interests that are either opposed to those of the New Criticism or are beyond its ken. Thus deconstructionists, for example, read a text in order to show the impossibility of reading it as an organic whole. Structuralists and deconstructionists alike disintegrate the text and connect elements of it with the elements of other texts to constitute an intertextuality. (The very idea of intertextuality erodes generic distinctions among texts.) Contemporary literary speculation in its various versions is opposed to New Critical assumptions about the autonomy, uniqueness, and objectivity of individual texts.

Where Arnold is concerned, the difference is of a metaphysical order. If, as Paul de Man tells us, "true literary consciousness . . . never results from the absence of something, but consists of the presence of a nothingness," Arnold's enterprise would appear to be wholly misconceived. Deconstructionists deny the faith, not from empiricist premises, but from a counterfaith in the void. For Arnold true literary consciousness is the attempt to restore our perception of divine origins, which a dogmatic and literalizing religion has obscured. When he takes Arnold to task for trying to turn art into religion, the poet of *Four Quartets* does not deny a transcendental or religious function to literature. Eliot's criticism is directed against what he sees as Arnold's misunderstanding of the proper relationship between art and religion. Most contemporary practitioners of literary criticism and scholarship have avoided questions about the relationship between art and religion; Arnold as a literary and religious thinker does not speak to them. But the open philosophical atheism of deconstruction does speak against our Arnoldian legacy. If we resist deconstruction, it is because of a residual instinctive commitment to literary value, which has been given its most powerful expression in the English tradition by Arnold. If we try to raise that commitment to intellectual consciousness, we are embarrassed by the order of piety that such consciousness seems to exude.

Arnold in our time has been an emblem of what might be called a concern with the social question of the humanities. The territory of concern goes beyond our educational institutions, including, as it must, our political and moral lives. In disabling the humanist perspective, contemporary skeptics see themselves not as willful destroyers but as rigorous truthseekers. (In the interests of truth, even truth becomes suspect.) In their view, it is futile to regret what is no longer possible. Of course, no amount of deconstructive skepticism can dissolve the need to remedy illiteracy, or to criticize political and moral falsehood, or to discriminate between a successful and failed work of art, though to the extent that deconstruction is persuasive, it may dissolve the will to satisfy the need.

2

THE TRANSCENDENTAL SITE: FROM HEAVEN TO EARTH

There is an unintended irony in Arnold's view of romanticism as deficient in ideas. It was, after all, romanticism that made the greatest contribution to Arnold's principal idea: the relocation of the transcendental site from heaven to earth. The idea is the legacy of both English and German romanticism, and studies of its literary consequences can be found in, among other works, Georg Lukács's *The Theory of the Novel* (1920) and Meyer Abrams's *Natural Supernaturalism* (1971), which provides an account of lyric poetry remarkably similar to Lukács's account of the novel. In their most ambitious moods, the novel and the lyric poem in the nineteenth century aspire to become epic, the literary form that tries to encompass all of experience. This aspiration may not always name itself as religious, but its narrative structure unmistakably discloses its religious motive.

The romantics reconceived Christian providential history in secular terms. The myths of prelapsarian man, the Fall, and the possibility of redemption give direction to the March of Progress. In *Natural Supernaturalism*, Abrams explains and fully documents the process of secularization. What emerges from his exposition is an idea that has a particular narrative form with implications for both history and imaginative fiction. The fable that underlies the nineteenth-century narrative is the parable of the Prodigal Son who leaves his father and squanders his fortune (as Adam squandered Paradise), only to return after the ordeal of loss and estrangement to his home and reconcile himself with his father, often through the mediation of a female figure. The reconciliation symbolizes a regaining of a Paradise greater than the one that was lost. Again and again Christian writers retrace the circuitous journey of the Prodigal Son. In the words of St. Augustine, men after the Fall see themselves as "strangers and pilgrims on the earth. For they that say such things declare plainly that they seek a country. And truly, if they had been mindful of that country from whence they came out, they might have had opportunity to have returned. But now they desire a better country, that is, an heavenly: wherefore God is not ashamed to be called their God: for he has prepared for them a city."[1]

The structure is pervasively present not only in imaginative literature, but in philosophical literature as well. As Abrams shows, Hegel's dialectic is in essence a secular reworking of the scriptural parable of the Prodigal Son. Hegel had inherited the narrative form of his philosophy from Jacob Boehme, for whom "a first principle becomes creative by generating its own contrary, which it then proceeds to reconcile to itself."[2] Like the parable of the Prodigal Son, Hegel's (and Boehme's) story is of an historical journey which assumes a beginning (an origin) and conclusive return (i.e., reconciliation) after a middle period of conflict and suffering. The story begins with a vulnerable plenitude, unfolds through loss, separation, and emptiness only to recover a greater and more secure sense of fullness and harmony. The story may move through a series of reconciliations, each vulnerable to further division and conflict, with the final reconciliation in which the dialectic totalizes the contradictory elements that have entered into its process.

In his examination of Wordsworth's *Prelude*, Keats's *Fall*

[1] Quoted in M. H. Abrams, *Natural Supernaturalism: Tradition and Revolution in Romantic Literature* (New York: W. W. Norton, 1971), p. 164.

[2] Ibid., p. 162.

of Hyperion, Carlyle's *Sartor Resartus*, and Hölderlin's *Hyperion*, among other "epic works," Abrams reveals the dialectical structure that they all have. For example:

> In the course of his narrated life from infancy into manhood, Hyperion moves through stages of experience in which he periodically seems to approach a lost consonance with himself and with the outer world; at each stage, however, the equilibrium proves unstable and at once divides into opposites that press in turn toward a new integration. Hyperion passes through the Edenic self-unity of childhood, in the peace and happiness before the child "has come to be at odds with itself," and before "Nature drives it out of its Paradise."[3]

The dialectic of division, union, and further division continues, finally to be resolved "in a Wordsworthian way, after a mental crisis and the discovery of a rationale for seeming evil, with a union between the disalienated mind and a rehumanized nature."[4] Abrams's sense of dialectical resolution is a bit too comfortable, especially in light of Fichte's view, which Abrams himself says is characteristic: "the ultimate goal of man . . . is utterly unattainable . . . his way to it must be endless."[5]

Abrams's account is limited by his virtually single-minded attention to lyric poetry that aspires to the condition of the epic: *The Prelude*, the *Hyperions*, Shelley's *Prometheus Unbound*, Blake's *Jerusalem*. This is understandable, given the fact that an epically inspired lyric poetry has been the chief glory of romanticism. Lukács had earlier discovered the aspiration toward what Hegel called totality in the novel, the literary form of "transcendental homelessness." The greatest novels characteristically aspire and fail to reach the transcendental site where all conflicts are resolved. The

[3] Ibid., p. 239.
[4] Ibid., p. 241.
[5] Ibid., p. 216.

novel is a fragment that dreams wholeness. The epic, in Lukács's argument, represents a world in which meaning is everywhere immanent. There is no division between essence and accident that one finds in classical drama, or between a fallen world and a transcendental site in the beyond that one finds in Dante, the poet of a Christian epic. The catastrophic division that Lukács seems to postulate between the ancient Greek world in which meaning is everywhere immanent and the godless modern world that has been emptied of meaning is compromised by symptoms of division within the ancient world itself. Whatever the historical truth of Lukács's conception of epic reality, it functions as a utopian object of desire in his argument.

The modern desire for epic totality is a Faustian desire, which can never be satisfied.

> Our world has become infinitely large and each of its corners is richer in gifts and dangers than the world of the Greeks, but such wealth cancels out the positive meaning—upon which their life was based. For totality as the formative prime reality of every individual phenomenon implies that something closed within itself can be completed; completed because everything occurs within it ripens to its own perfection and, by attaining itself, submits to limitation. Totality of being is possible only where everything is already homogeneous before it has been contained by forms; where forms are not a constraint but only the becoming conscious, the coming to the surface of everything that has been lying dormant as a vague longing in the innermost depths of that which had to be given form; where knowledge is virtue and virtue happiness, where beauty is the meaning of the world made visible.[6]

Lukács's *Theory of the Novel* describes the ambition and the failure of the novel to achieve totality. "The novel gener-

[6] Georg Lukács, *The Theory of the Novel*, trans. Anna Bostock (Cambridge, Mass.: MIT Press, 1971), p. 34.

ically seeks and fails to find the essence."[7] Ideas fail to "penetrate reality," making it "heterogeneous and discrete."[8] The hero of the novel looks to return to the transcendental site of his origins, but his condition is one of "transcendental homelessness."[9] The soul's demand for communion with "an outside world" is utopian.[10] "In a novel, totality can be systematized only in abstract terms."[11] Yet the very meaning of division, fragmentation, failure in the novel, in Lukács's account, depends upon the desire to overcome them. The great novels of the nineteenth century may fail to achieve epic totality, but their greatness consists in their refusal to accept defeat. The novels of Balzac and Tolstoy, among others, may not incorporate all of nineteenth-century reality, but they create the illusion of a world "closed and ordered within itself." Their strong narratives encompass an enormous wealth of social and personal detail. One has the impression of the development of character and world to the greatest possible fullness.

Yet there are significant differences between the prodigal sons of the nineteenth-century novels and the Prodigal Son of scripture. In the novels of the nineteenth century (e.g., *Great Expectations, Wuthering Heights*), homes are not places where children enjoy innocence and security. The journey from home is an escape from guilt and oppression. If the nineteenth-century prodigal experiences "transcendental homelessness," the home that awaits him at the end of the journey seems like an unreal utopian invention, manufactured out of the character's need and the novelist's supportive imagination (e.g., *Bleak House*).

In his discussion of Lukács, Fredric Jameson perceives an unresolved contradiction in *The Theory of the Novel*. ". . . We find Lukács describing the hero's quest as an attempt

[7] Ibid., p. 122.
[8] Ibid., p. 80.
[9] Ibid., p. 41.
[10] Ibid., p. 144.
[11] Ibid., p. 70.

to 'prove his soul' (Browning), to overcome the primal homesickness of being by 'returning home' in a metaphysical sense (Novalis: 'Immer nach Hause!') by reintegrating that 'transcendental site' which was the original dwelling of the soul. . . ." Yet this is incompatible with "Lukács' formal description of the novel as a process in which no guidelines are given in advance, in which, therefore, even this characterization of man's metaphysical quest in the world is not permissible, and stands as preconceived value imposed on the initial formlessness of existence."[12] But the quest is impermissible only if one censors the desire for reconciliation and unity with the transcendental site. Jameson's judgment in effect abolishes the experience of fragmentation (which in turn depends at the very least on an imagined experience of wholeness) in behalf of a modern anti-metaphysical presupposition of "the initial formlessness of existence," a presupposition he claims to find in Lukács himself.

The nineteenth-century idea of totalization can be extended to the classic modernists Proust and Joyce, though it is significantly modified by pressure from an increasing awareness of "the initial formlessness of existence." The hero's attempt "to prove his soul" and to return home ("the transcendental site") occurs in time. Time, in which the present moment links past and future, is the ambiguous medium of growing and decaying, healing and destruction. But when time becomes exclusively the medium of decay and destruction, when it no longer nourishes and ceases to promise development or fulfillment, it becomes a bondage to the imagination.

In *Remembrance of Things Past*, Proust expresses disdain for "the present scene," which denies access to the only source of happiness—the past. Proust's scorn for "actual life" is unmitigated—not because Proust thinks of himself as cursed like Kafka, deficient in his capacity for life, but

[12] Fredric Jameson, *Marxism and Form* (Princeton: Princeton University Press, 1971), p. 179.

because he believes he has discovered in the very conditions of living the insufficiency and painfulness of the present: "social pleasures, which at best produce the discomfort caused by partaking of wretched food; or friendship, which is a delusion, because, for whatever moral reasons he may do it, the artist who gives up an hour of work for an hour's conversation with a friend knows that he is sacrificing a reality for something which is non-existent." If the present is empty, it nonetheless has the force of repression, which turns the scene of involuntary memory into a battleground in which "the resurrections of the past are usually vanquished—though they seem more beautiful than the victory." In this battle, Proust perceives his vocation as an artist: to perpetuate the "timelessness" of these past moments in art. This is achieved by what Proust characterizes as a suspension of the harsh law by which the imagination normally operates. Proust describes the miraculous moment (which occurs to Marcel on a visit to the Duke of Guermantes) in the following way:

> And now suddenly the operation of this harsh law was neutralized, suspended, by a miraculous expedient of nature by which a sensation—the sound of the spoon and that of the hammer, a similar unevenness in two paving stones—was reflected both in the past (which made it possible for my imagination to take pleasure in it) and in the present, the physical stimulus of the sound or the contact with the stones adding to the dreams of the imagination that which they usually lack, the idea of existence—and this subterfuge made it possible for the being within me to seize, isolate, immobilize for the duration of a lightening flash what it never apprehends, namely, a fragment of time in its pure state.

The seductiveness of this victory makes us almost forget its extraordinary conditions: an absolute hostility to the present, the abolition of present life, and the absolutizing and separating of the fragmentary moment from the real life in which it is embedded. Nevertheless, the "fragmentary" moment is not a single moment of chronological time. As Gerard Genette has demonstrated in his superb study of narrative discourse, Proust achieves a kind of permanent unity of experience through "the iterative syllepsis": the use of the imperfect tense enables Proust to synthesize "similar events" by abolishing their succession. The synthesis, to be sure, does not incorporate all the moments of Proust's experience and in that sense remains fragmentary, but the grammar, so to speak, of Proust's imagination confers a unity on what are chronologically discrete moments of experience. This unity is the consequence of retrospection. Episodes that at the moment of their occurence were empty of significance are later "suddenly reassembled, now made significant by being bound together among themselves" in the consciousness of the hero Marcel.[13] The synthesizing activity is the involuntary work of memory abetted by art. The mimetic truth in Proust's rendering of the work of memory produces in the reader the shock of recognition. All of us (artists and nonartists alike) have experienced in life those moments in which past experiences converge into significance. But for nonartists those moments are themselves transient. It is the artist with his superior powers of attention and articulation (in the double sense of expression and the making of connections) who can perpetuate the privileged moment.

This capacity of memory and art, which *The Remembrance of Things Past* enacts and celebrates, would seem to be an instance of totalization. "The subject of the *Recherche* [Genette remarks] is indeed 'Marcel becomes a writer': *Recherche* remains a novel of development. . . ."[14] But with this difference: the development of the would-be artist to the point of artistic consciousness, the assumption of the vo-

[13] Gerard Genette, *Narrative Discourse*, trans. Jane E. Lewin (Ithaca, N.Y.: Cornell University Press, 1979), p. 56.

[14] Ibid., p. 227.

cation of the artist, does not correspond to the full development of the self. The future does not develop and differ from past and present because there is no present and there is only a past to be recaptured and joined to other pasts. The distance between the recapturing consciousness and the past has no chronological interest (though there is a distance in time): it occurs in a timeless space. Marcel is not transformed or changed by his discovered artistic consciousness. In this sense, what is recovered, or, perhaps more accurately, created, is a partial plenitude dissociated from organic ideas of growth and development.

Leo Bersani has argued that contemporary literature celebrates "marginal or partial selves, or to put it another way, a disseminated scattered self which resists all efforts to make a unifying structure of fragmented desire."[15] He notes that in the nineteenth century there was "an aesthetic of completeness" in which art was not conceived and experienced at the expense of an active and effective participation in (present) life. According to Bersani, Proust equivocates between two views: one view is that the unity is intrinsic to Balzac's *La Comédie Humaine* and Wagner's tetralogy, the other is that it is an invention of the artist, "imposing upon the work retrospectively a unity, a greatness which it does not possess." Though Proust acknowledged that unity was after the fact, he judged it, in Genette's words, "not fictitious, perhaps indeed all the more real for being ulterior, for being born of a moment of enthusiasm where it is discovered to exist among fragments which need only to be joined together. A unity that has been unaware of itself, therefore vital and not logical, that has not banned variety, chilled execution."[16] Nevertheless, Proust may have underestimated "the fragments' resistance to being 'joined together.' "

[15] Leo Bersani, *Baudelaire and Freud* (Berkeley and Los Angeles: University of California Press, 1977), p. 132.

[16] Genette, *Narrative Discourse*, p. 149.

In any event, Proust boldly faced the problem of unity in the presence of fragmentation both in the work of art and in the conception of the self. The "fulfillment" of the "I" in Proust does not consist in the totalization of experience; it is rather at certain privileged moments coextensive with the fragmentary absolute that sprang from the past and that contains, as we have seen, a certain richness and even unity. Proust's imagination makes the journey home, but it is not the journey through time in which the self is reconstituted at a higher level after the divisions, the self-estrangements of experience. What he recovers is not self or wholeness but a fragment of the self incarnated and absolutized by memory.

For Stephen Dedalus in Joyce's *Ulysses*, the dream of totalization is baffled by time, which excludes more than it includes.

> time has branded them . . . They are lodged in the infinite possibilities they have ousted. But can those have been possible seeing that they never were? Or was that only possible which came to pass?

In a subsequent conversation with the schoolmaster Mr. Deasy (in the same episode, the Nestor episode), Stephen states his personal anguish in world-historical terms.

> —History . . . is a nightmare from which I am trying to awake.
>
> From the playfield the boys raised a shout. A whirring whistle: goal. What if the nightmare gave you a back kick?
>
> —The ways of the Creator are not our ways, Mr. Deasy said. All history moves toward one great goal, the manifestation of God,
>
> Stephen jerked his thumb towards the window, saying:
>
> —That is God.
>
> Hooray! Ay! Whrrwhee!
>
> —What? Mr. Deasy asked.
>
> —A shout in the street, Stephen answered, shrugging his shoulders.

In repudiating providential history, Stephen rejects a selective mimesis that excludes the contingencies and accidents of life. He wants to achieve an incorporation (without discrimination) of everything that exists, the transient noises, the unenacted possibilities of the imagination.

The artistic will to incorporate all of reality is dissembled in a modern writer like Joyce by the mask of impersonality. Stephen Dedalus may climb Mt. Olympus, leaving his creation behind him, or he may "disappear" into the narrative itself, but only a literal belief in the dogma of impersonality will prevent us from experiencing the all-powerful presence of the artistic will. The impersonality of the artist is a Faustian personality and becomes the "world" in all its multiplicity and heterogeneity. In its impersonal form, the artistic will enjoys a freedom that it never had as a merely "personal" will. This Faustian will to encompass paradoxically respects the heterogeneity, the openness, and the endlessness of the world.

I have extended the nineteenth-century idea of totalization to the classic modernists Proust and Joyce against Lukács's own understanding of modernism. For Lukács the modern imagination luxuriates in its fragmentation: it has no faith in the power of the will (joined to the social process) to change the world or society through incorporation. (Jameson acutely notes how a shift occurs within *The Theory of the Novel* from the metaphysical term "world" to the historical term "society."[17]) The displacement of the totalizing impulse from society to art can only generate illusions in Lukács's view, since art (or Art) that thinks of itself as a self-sufficient world (a totality) is no more than a fragment of a greater world.

In a discussion of what he calls the "two realisms" of the modern period, Erich Heller addresses himself to the modern artist's will to incorporate reality. The first type is "the absolute poetic imperialism" of nineteenth-century romantic writers (Stendhal, Balzac, Flaubert, Dostoevsky, Tolstoy)

[17] Jameson, *Marxism and Form*, pp. 180-81.

who envisaged the conquest by poetry of every human activity, "religion, science, politics." This type of realism is paralleled by the work of Hegel, who conceived the project of imperial conquest for philosophical understanding. The second type of realism is the work of the writers (Baudelaire, Mallarmé, Rimbaud, Valéry, Rilke) who offer a realism that is, in Flaubert's words, "without any external connection, and . . . would support itself entirely by the internal force of style."[18] As Heller explains, "now external reality has no claims any more to being real. The only real world is the world of human inwardness." Heller assigns the word "realism" both to the first enterprise, because of its "passion of understanding, the desire for rational appropriation, the driving force towards the expropriation of the mystery" that he finds in the pages of Stendhal, Balzac et al. and to the second enterprise, because of its claim to possess (in its art) greater reality than what is familiarly considered to be real. Flaubert is in a sense the mediating figure between the two realisms. He "was dismayed by the undue resistance offered by reality, although there were times when he modestly believed that the rational penetration of the real world could suffice." Heller gives as instances of the second type of realism *Ulysses, Finnegans Wake*, and Broch's *The Death of Vergil.* The distinction is not so sharp as Heller would make it. In *Ulysses*, for instance, the external world is absorbed into the inwardness, the subjectivities of the characters in a way that suggests the poetic imperialism of the first type of realism. The will to conquer persists, but in the earlier attempts external reality was worth conquering because, for all its corruption, it remained substantial, whereas later writers (Joyce is an ambiguous instance), having devalued external reality, had in effect already conquered or believed to have conquered it.

[18] "The Realistic Fallacy: A Discussion of Realism in Literature," in *Documents of Modern Literary Realism*, ed. George J. Becker (Princeton: Princeton University Press, 1963), pp. 597-98.

Difficult as it might be, the desire to encompass, to give order, to reality is inextinguishable. Hayden White admits as much, even in his demystification of the effort: "The value attached to narrativity in representation of real events arises out of a desire to have real events display the coherence, integrity, fullness and closure of an image of life that can only be imaginary."[19] In White's description of annals and chronicles (the alternative to teleological narrative) we have a version of the devalued external reality that Heller speaks of. White asks: "Does the world really represent itself to perception in the form of well-made stories, with central subjects, proper beginnings, middles and ends, and a coherence that permits us to see the end in every beginning? Or does it present itself more in the forms that the annals and chronicles suggest, either as mere sequence without beginning or end or as sequences of beginnings that only terminate and never conclude?" For White, a post-structuralist, the answer is clear: The world presents itself "in the form of annals and chronicles." The teleological shaping narrative impulse, whether in history or in fiction, is suspect in its claims to realism. Implicit in White's view is Nietzsche's radical distinction between "the world of aims" and "the realm of nature and of necessity."

> Intelligence is justified in a world of aims. But if it is true our aims are only a sort of rumination of experiences in which the actual agent remains hidden, we are not entitled to transfer purposeful systems of action into the nature of things. This means that there is no need to imagine intelligence as capable of representation. Intelligence can only exist in a world in which mistakes occur, in which *error reigns*—a world of consciousness. In the realm of nature and of necessity, all teleological hypotheses are absurd. Necessity means that there can only be one possibility. Why then do we have to assume the

[19] Hayden White, "The Value of Narrativity," *Critical Inquiry* 7 (Autumn 1980), 27.

> presence of an intellect in the realm of things?—And if the will cannot be conceived without implying its representation, the "will" is not an adequate expression for the core of nature either.[20]

White displaces the opposition from intelligence versus nature to historical narrative versus real history, a somewhat misleading displacement, since history, unlike nature, is in the realm of possibility and purpose. In any event, totality is a result of teleological thinking, the attempt to incorporate into a coherent whole all of human and natural reality.

It matters greatly whether one stresses the persistence of the totalizing impulse in the work of Proust and Joyce or its "deconstruction." The "message" of *The Remembrance of Things Past* and *Ulysses* may be that totality is an impossible, indeed an intolerable, dream: a "monster" in Roland Barthes's characterization. Yet what is this monster, but an enormously exaggerated projection of desire: transcendence imposed on the small space of the actual. Coherence, fullness, unity, continuity: the value terms that have their source in the transcendent space became *over*valued in the nineteenth century in the (always) premature desire to realize transcendence in the actual world. Totalization is the hubristic attempt to transform the small circle of values and convictions into a triumphant movement.

Eliot may have sensed hubris of this kind in Arnold's conflation of culture and religion. The hubris, however, is strongly qualified, if not contradicted, by Arnold's view that criticism never achieves the finality of triumph, that the process of making and asserting its values is or should be endless. It is an interesting fact (and insufficiently remarked) that the totalizing hubristic legacy of Arnold persists in some of Eliot's New Critical followers—as, for example, in John Crowe Ransom's tribute to the poetic source of religion:

[20] Quoted in Paul de Man, *Allegories of Reading* (New Haven: Yale University Press, 1979), p. 100.

> From the strict point of view of literary criticism it must be insisted that the miraculism which produces the humblest conceit is the same miraculism which supplies to religions their substantive content. (This is said to assert the dignity not of the conceits but of the religions.) It is the poet and nobody else who gives to the God a nature, a form, faculties, and a history; to the God, most comprehensive of all terms, which if there were no poetic impulse to actualize or "find" Him, would remain the driest and deadest among Platonic ideas, with all intension sacrificed to infinite extension. The myths are conceits, born of metaphors. Religions are periodically produced by poets and destroyed by naturalists. Religion depends for its ontological validity upon a literary understanding, and that is why it is frequently misunderstood.[21]

Ransom's characterization of the "ontological validity" of religion could become a demystification of religion, but Ransom clearly intends to resist such an interpretation in his parenthetical remark: "This is said to assert the dignity not of the conceits but of the religions." Earlier in his essay, Ransom notes that "the meaning of metaphysical which was common in Dryden's time, having come down in the Middle Ages through Shakespeare was simply: supernatural, miraculous."[22] The miraculous to which Ransom refers is the human capacity for metaphor, the essential activity of poetic language and the source of its religious aura. In Ransom we are beyond Arnold's sense of criticism (in his modest mood) as an underminer of triumphant movements.

Even Northrop Frye, who introduces a scientific ambition into literary study, remains an heir of the Arnoldian legacy. Indeed, science, in Frye's view, may be no more than a theological instrument to articulate the plenitude of literature as a whole. For Frye, as for Arnold, the space of

[21] John Crowe Ransom, *The World's Body* (New York and London: Charles Scribner's Sons, 1938), p. 140.

[22] Ibid., p. 133.

imagination is a transcendent space. "The imaginative element of works of art . . . lifts them clear of the bondage of history."[23] The advent of structuralism, remote from the Arnoldian legacy, preserves the totalizing ambition of romanticism to discover in the human mind structures that unify all of existence.

The consciousness of totality as presence and obstacle is peculiar to post-structuralism. The desire of post-structuralists to shatter totality, to break form and empty the text has more than one motive. It declares itself in behalf of truth. One may paraphrase Harold Bloom: "the sad truth is that totality is a lie, form is an arbitrary metaphor." It declares itself as freedom. Totality is an oppression, extinguishing desire. Truth and freedom are now the expression of a new atheism. Emptiness and nothingness become, so to speak, anti-god terms. They are counterparts in their extremity and purity to the oversized fullness of the totalizing language of nineteenth-century thought.

Freedom and truth are by no means absolute or secure terms in post-structuralist discourse. In the deconstructive version, necessity is often stronger than freedom; indeed, freedom may be an illusion. But in its combat with totality, liberation is the order of the day. The "liberation" occurs in various ways. Fiction is not obligated to the teleological order of plot; discourse need not concern itself with logical coherence. (In this perspective, teleology, which Nietzsche says belongs to the human realm of possibility, not the natural realm of necessity, hardens into necessity. If *telos* can be conceived as "opening itself,"[24] it can also be viewed

[23] Frye, *Anatomy of Criticism* (Princeton: Princeton University Press, 1957), p. 347.

[24] Jacques Derrida, *Writing and Difference*, trans. Alan Bass (Chicago: University of Chicago Press, 1978), p. 167. The passage in which the phrase appears is the following: "Since *telos* is totally open, is opening itself, to say that it is the most powerful a priori historicity is not to designate it as a static and determined value which would inform and enclose the genesis of Being and meaning. It is the concrete possibility,

in its realization as a constraining closure.) The "artificial" bonds of selfhood are sundered and the self dissolves into the authentic flux or discontinuity of experience. Language is severed between the signifier and the signified, and the signifier multiplies "meanings" or the simulacrum of meanings, which diverge from one another in purposeless play.

The "liberation" occurs essentially through the discovery of linguistics as an instrument for demystification and desacralization. Jacques Derrida follows the linguistics of Saussure when he speaks of language as a system of differences without positive or substantial terms. In Derrida's hands, difference will become an instrument of dissemination, in which the structures of discourse that we take for granted are shown to be founded on nothing. The impulse to demystify and disseminate is provoked and marked by the very excess of the totalizing ambition of the nineteenth century. The post-structuralist combat is in terms of all or nothing.

---

the very birth of history and the meaning of becoming in general. Therefore it is structurally genesis itself, as origin and as becoming." Derrida wants to free thought from the constraints of origins, but he understands as fully as any advocate of teleology its open and dynamic aspect.

3

ROLAND BARTHES AND THE MONSTER OF TOTALITY

The work of Roland Barthes is pivotal in the history of post-structuralism, for it is marked by an incompletely resolved ambivalence toward "the monster of totality." This ambivalence shows itself in his career as a demystifier.

In the preface to *Mythologies* (1957) Roland Barthes warns us that demystification is "a word which is beginning to show signs of wear." We hardly need to be reminded that for Marx, as it had been for the thinkers of the Enlightenment, demystification was the very essence of criticism. All criticism, Marx had written in an early essay, was the criticism of religion: the clearing of the religious mists that conceal the sun of truth. Much later in his career when he writes the celebrated chapter on commodity fetishism in *Capital*, Marx finds an analogy for the mystifications of the commodity world in the "mist-filled regions" of the religious life.

Demystification in the nineteenth century was a radical expression of the secularizing spirit. Its energy was employed in the interest of a substantial truth, which was concealed by false religious expressions. (For others, like Carlyle, religious expressions were symbols of truth and did not need to be demystified.) The desire to discover and reconstitute the substantial truth of things, concealed by the veil of false or seductive appearances, can be found in Marx's attack on the young Hegelians, who were primarily interested in destruction.

> Criticism has plucked the imaginary flowers from the chains not so that man may bear chains without any imagination or comfort, but so that he may throw away the chains and pluck the living flowers. The criticism of religion disillusions man so that he may think, act, and fashion his own reality as a disillusioned man comes to his senses; so that he may revolve around himself as his real sun.[1]

Seen in its negative aspect, demystification is a destructive process. But it may also be seen as an analogue or even a mode of secularization, a dispelling of the mists, the excrescences, the obstacles (the imagery may vary) that prevent us from experiencing the truth. Demystification may be another name for the dialectical process, which breaks up false unities in order (after struggle) to elicit authentic ones. Or, at least, this is the nineteenth-century legacy of demystification. Thus in the chapter on commodity fetishism, Marx could penetrate the false pretensions of commodities to an "existence as independent beings endowed with life, which entered into relations with one another and the human race," because he was confident that behind the illusion the real value of the product was ascertainable: the labor expended in its production. And it is not simply the truth or the conviction of truth that Marx possessed. The reality to which the truth corresponded was substantial and filled with promise, for the labor theory of value becomes the justification for the socialist revolution. Demystification may expose a corrupt reality—for example, the exploitation of the working class concealed in the exchange of commodities in the marketplace—but such a reality is substantial and, moreover, contains within it the dialectical possibility of progress to a condition that restores to the worker the product of his labor.

But if there is no reality behind illusion, then to "pene-

[1] Quoted in David McLellan, *Karl Marx: His Life and Thought* (London: Macmillan, 1973), p. 90.

trate the object," is, as Barthes put it, not to liberate it but to destroy it. Demystification for Barthes shows signs of wear because, necessary as it may be, it cannot satisfy the appetite for wholeness, for substantiality, for presence as it did for Marx. "We constantly drift between the object and its demystification, powerless to render its wholeness," Barthes declares almost poignantly at the end of a book apparently devoted to demystification.[2] Barthes contemplates the prospect of the present scene, which has been emptied out—without the resources of Proust's miraculous past. In *Mythologies* he betrays a nineteenth-century appetite for wholeness or reconciliation, but, as I will show, he has no confidence in the possibility of achieving it.

Unlike Marx (who in this respect is typical of the nineteenth century) Barthes does not possess a vision of reality alternative to the myths that he demystifies and, consequently, from which he excludes himself. His "impatience at the sight of the 'naturalness' with which newspapers, art, and common-sense dress up reality,"[3] does not presuppose an authentic nature that the contemporary world betrays. Nature has several meanings and anti-meanings, and they all figure in Barthes's rejection of the possibility of the natural world: the real as opposed to the illusory, the normal opposed to the abnormal, the innocent to the corrupt, the artless to the artificial. In *Roland Barthes by Roland Barthes* (1975), Barthes, reflecting on a theme that has preoccupied him from the beginning of his career, opposes history to nature and claims for history the power of relativizing nature and making it possible "to believe in meaning in time." In contrast, nature oppressively makes all things motionless, eternal: "like milk spoiled in the disintegrated space of phraseology."[4] This, of course, recalls a Marxian dis-

[2] Roland Barthes, *Mythologies*, trans. Annette Lavers (New York: Hill & Wang, 1957), p. 159.

[3] Ibid., p. 11.

[4] *Roland Barthes by Roland Barthes*, trans. Richard Howard (New York: Hill & Wang, 1977), p. 126.

tinction, but the distinction does not provide Barthes with the experience of an alternative plenitude to the empty abstractions of bourgeois nature. For Marx, history was a natural force comparable to the evolutionary system described by Darwin. All that remains of the natural in Barthes is the honesty of acknowledging that innocence is no longer possible, a purely negative condition, immensely difficult to sustain.

In a remarkable essay on La Rochefoucauld, Barthes examines a particular method of demystification. Through a series of maxims, La Rochefoucauld reduces heroism to ambition, ambition to jealousy, and finally jealousy to "the grandest of all passions (*amour propre*)." Barthes presses beyond *amour propre*. "When the ultimate passion has been designated, this passion too vanishes away, it can be nothing but sloth, inertia, nothingness."[5] According to Barthes, La Rochefoucauld has immobilized the process in the maxim, which can be demystified in grammatical terms as a reduction engendered by *ne que*. ("*L'hëroisme n'est que l'ambition.*" Heroism is only ambition.) As Barthes wittily remarks, "The pessimism of La Rochefoucauld is only an incomplete rationalism."[6] Beyond or underneath the classical "clarity" of La Rochefoucauld's pessimism is the modern *néant*. One wonders, however, whether in completing the rational process, Barthes is not participating in the universalist Cartesian assumption of a rational and natural sequence of events. The *néant* is as opaque, as arbitrary, as unnatural as any other cultural sign that can be demystified. Barthes implicitly makes it the only real or natural term in his discourse—despite his relentless explicit denials of all claims to naturalness. How would Barthes accommodate the possibly irreducible experience of plenitude in the lives and works of Wordsworth, Tolstoy, and Lawrence? Barthes

[5] Roland Barthes, *New Critical Essays*, trans. Richard Howard (New York: Hill & Wang, 1980), p. 18.

[6] Ibid., p. 11.

simply makes the parochial assumption that La Rochefoucauld's method of demystification, abortive as it is, is the only route that demystification can take: the route to the *vide*, the *néant*.

I don't mean to say that the presence of the *néant* in Barthes always reflects a Cartesian bias. As I show later, it also springs from Barthes's affinity for the Marxist analysis of capitalism. The Cartesian assumption and the Marxist view become mutually reinforcing. But what I want to stress is the illicit way in which the *néant* has been exempt from a scrutiny that discovers arbitrariness and artificiality in every other term. The *néant* is, in the sequence of demystification, a deduction or a move in a game whose principal rule is expressed by the syntactical form *ne que*. As Kenneth Burke pointed out more than two decades ago, Heidegger and Sartre had reified Nothing into a metaphysical "substance." Because that substance is called Nothing, it had eluded the kind of skeptical scrutiny that other claims to metaphysical existence have received. It should also be pointed out that though Barthes cunningly uncovers the linguistic formula of demystification, the reductionist *ne que*, he doesn't challenge it as a mode of thought. All he says of La Rochefoucauld is that he has not gone far enough in the process of reduction.

Kenneth Burke has remarked that the reductionist habit is "to treat 'higher' concepts in terms of 'lower' ones," a pattern which, as Burke notes, goes back as far as the maxims of La Rochefoucauld, "which treat 'virtues' in terms of 'vices.' "[7] Barthes *de*moralizes the movement of reduction, seeing it rather as ontological. The movement is from delusive substance to nothingness. If the terms of reduction differ in Barthes from what they are in La Rochefoucauld, the movement and motive are the same. It would be wrong to include Marx in this account, precisely because Marxism

[7] Kenneth Burke, *A Grammar of Motives* (Englewood Cliffs, N.J.: Prentice-Hall, 1952), p. 97.

has the *dialectical* capacity to convert the "reduction" into an enhancement. In reducing the commodity from the magical scene of the marketplace to the prosaic productive space of labor, Marx does not diminish the commodity. Rather he returns it to its productive source and in doing so reminds the working class of its revolutionary potential. The Marxist reduction produces an increase in (class) consciousness.

The term reductionism may be given too broad an application. It is, I think, misleading to lump all demystifiers together under a single heading as Paul Ricoeur does when he characterizes them as "protagonists of suspicion" in the following terms:

> The contemporary philosopher meets Freud on the same ground as Nietzsche and Marx. All three rise before him as protagonists of suspicion who rip away masks and pose the novel problem of the lie of consciousness and consciousness as a lie. This problem cannot remain just one among many, for what all three generally and radically put into question is something that appears to any good phenomenologist as the field, foundation, and very origin of any meaning at all: consciousness itself.[8]

It is one thing to dispel false consciousness in favor of true consciousness as Marx does or means to do; it is another thing to dispel the very truth of consciousness (i.e., to see "consciousness as a lie") as Nietzsche does. But it is true that both modes of demystification put into question the phenomenological field of experience. We are taught by demystifiers of whatever persuasion never to trust the immediacy of experience.

By repudiating nature as a given in human experience, Barthes, who is exemplary of post-existentialist thought in this respect, has implicitly assumed the alternative ade-

[8] Paul Ricoeur, *The Conflict of Interpretations: Essays in Hermeneutics*, ed. Don Ihde (Evanston, Ill.: Northwestern University Press, 1974), p. 99.

quacy of culture or history as a source of human values. What undermines his assumption, however, is the sense of the arbitrariness of cultural or historical events. Every organization of human experience is provisional and questionably satisfactory. The authority of history as a legacy of the nineteenth century arose precisely from the fact that it was invested with the inevitable force of nature. If post-existentialists find in Marxism authority for the primacy of history over nature, they ignore or suppress Marx's essentialist view of history as a paradigm of human nature. Indeed, for this reason Marx can speak of the historical process as the medium in which humanity will fulfill itself. The sense of man and his products as radically indeterminate comes from the evacuation of nature from the historical process. On the nineteenth-century view, history is at once a relativizing and objectivizing activity. On the one hand, it undermines or relativizes the absolutisms of God and nature; on the other hand, it privileges or naturalizes events at any moment of time by giving them an objective status.

History for Marx, and Hegel before him, is the temporal medium in which values are articulated and enacted; it is the promise of transcendence. If, in Barthes's view, values are made by history, the demystifier's knowledge of history as a series of impermanent artificial structures unmakes those values. Whereas both Hegel and Marx could redeem the changefulness of history by conceiving its movement as progressive and cumulative, Barthes is left with the demystified sense of history as discrete and discontinuous structures, free of the totalizing laws of dialectical development. If Barthes seems to free history from the coercive inevitabilistic implications that one finds in Marx, he is susceptible to another kind of tyranny—that of chance and contingency, which human nature cannot resist since human nature has no existence.

From Barthes's perspective there is no firm ground on which to stand, no privileged position from which one can dispel illusions and pronounce the truth. "One cannot 'demystify' from the outside, in the name of ownership [note the connection between authority and demystification as traditionally understood], but one must steep oneself in the void one is revealing."[9] Barthes goes on to say of literature what could be said of the myths he treats. "Literature [in its indirection] is the very mode of the impossible, since it alone can speak its void, and by saying it, again establish a plenitude." One is tempted to linger on the word "impossible," for it is mystifying how literature establishes an authentic plenitude that itself does not invite demystification. One can only surmise that Barthes maintains a covert allegiance to literature as a privileged domain, so that all he has to do is to present the sign *literature* and trust it will carry the day. Barthes equivocates in his use of the term demystification between a view of the method as a process that issues in nothingness, and a view of the method that implies a reality alternative to mystification. His own method is sanctioned by the first view, but he is unhappy about its consequences (the reason for its showing signs of wear), and he tries to compensate for its destructiveness by arbitrarily claiming plenitude for literature.

In *Mythologies* Barthes admits that "he cannot see the Promised Land," by which he means that there is no natural or rational order that he can perceive through the present life of things as a basis for a utopian formation. Though he refuses to relinquish a hope for "tomorrow's positivity,"[10] the future remains a blank in his work. But that is not all. Having nothing but the present, the temptation to become an accomplice of the present is overwhelming. In characterizing Flaubert's intention in *Bouvard et Pecuchet* in *S/Z*, Barthes describes precisely the nature of his own relation to the myths of contemporary culture. "The writer's only control over stereotypic vertigo (this vertigo is also

[9] Barthes, *Critical Essays*, trans. Richard Howard (Evanston, Ill.: Northwestern University Press, 1972), p. 131.

[10] *Mythologies*, p. 157.

that of 'stupidity,' 'vulgarity,') is to participate in it without quotation marks, producing a text, not a parody." Since the function of writing, as Barthes conceives it, is "to make ridiculous, to annul the power (the intimidation) of one language over another, to dissolve any meta-language as soon as it is constituted,"[11] parody would be presumptuous. Barthes in effect ignores the usual warning about the danger of parody. It is said of the parodist that he risks being seduced by the thing he mocks. Parody ceases when the mockery forgets itself in celebration, or the celebration ceases to be pretense. In questioning the pretensions of parody, Barthes deliberately becomes a complicitous participant in the thing he parodies, or rather refuses to parody.

Before examining Barthes's complicity, a few examples of his method in treating contemporary myths would be useful.

> But what strikes one first in the mythology of the *jet man* is the elimination of speed: nothing in the legend alludes to this experience. We must here accept a paradox, which is in fact admitted by everyone with the greatest of ease, and even consumed as a proof of modernity. The paradox is that an excess of speed turns into repose.[12]

The paradox rests on the semantic trick of implicitly identifying speed with strenuous exertion. The important thing to note is the difference between demystification and paradox. In demystification, the thought moves from an illusory appearance to an opposite or subversive underlying truth. What Barthes gives us, however, is something quite different: two facts, or rather a fact (of speed) and an impression (of repose), are held together in an unresolved tension or in a perspective of alternative views.

"The mythology of Einstein shows him as a genius so

[11] Roland Barthes, *S/Z*, trans. Richard Miller (New York: Hill & Wang, 1974), p. 98.

[12] *Mythologies*, p. 71.

lacking in magic that one speaks about his thought as of a functional labour analogous to the mechanical making of sausages, the grinding of corn, or the crushing of ore."[13] Barthes provides us here with the sarcasm he earlier noted as the modern condition of truth. Having reduced the mythology of Einstein to the anti-magic of the machine, however, he restores magic to the machine, at once demystifying and mystifying the process. "Paradoxically" (a favorite word which Barthes understands in its primary, though archaic, meaning as *counter doxa*, against received belief), "the more the genius of the man was materialized under the guise of his brain, the more the product of his inventiveness came to acquire a magical dimension, and gave a new incarnation to the old esoteric image of a science entirely contained in a few letters" (the letters of the equation).

Still another instance, the article on striptease, provides us with a parable for the resistance to demystification that has become the paradoxical outcome of the logic of demystification. "Woman is desexualized at the moment when she is stripped naked."[14] The shedding of clothes yields emptiness. (Balzac's *Sarrasine*, which Barthes analyzes in *S/Z*, in its unveiling of the castrato Zambinella, is another parable of the process of demystification.)

Demystification is no longer the way by which one arrives at ultimate truth. It may itself be a strategy or tactic for a further mystification. How can we characterize Barthes's performance in the following passage? Is it the ultimate demystification of royalty, or is it a kind of tribute to the inexhaustible resourcefulness of royalty in sustaining its myth?

> . . . kings have a superhuman essence, and when they temporarily borrow certain forms of democratic life, it can only be through an incarnation which goes against nature, made possible through condescension alone: to

[13] Ibid., pp. 68-69.

[14] Ibid., p. 84.

flaunt the fact that kings are capable of prosaic actions is to recognize that this status is no more natural to them than angelism to common mortals, it is to acknowledge that the king is still king by divine right.[15]

The juxtaposition or contradiction between the sacred and the profane recurs continually in *Mythologies*. It does not, as one might expect, shatter the myth, but enhances it. Thus journalism itself becomes the source of a modern sense of miracle. "To endow the writer publicly with a good fleshly body, to reveal that he likes dry white wine and underdone steak, is to make even more miraculous for me, and of a more divine essence, the products of his art."[16] And again: "The spectacular alliance of so much nobility and so much futility means that one still believes in the contradiction: since it is totally miraculous, each of its terms is miraculous too; it would obviously lose all interest in a world where the writer's work was so desacralized that it appeared as natural as his vestimentary or gustatory functions."

The strategy of myth, as Barthes notes, is to admit the disadvantages of the value or product or institution presented. Having disarmed the skeptic by a pretense of honesty, the myth exalts the value of the product or the institution despite or because of the honesty. A divine art is created by a fleshly body. "A delicious food, tasty, digestible, economical, useful in all circumstances" is produced by the "fatty essence of oleomargarine."[17] The army as an object of devotion magically emerges from the experience of its cruel discipline (*From Here to Eternity*). Salvation comes to those who have mortified themselves by following the letter of the law, thus justifying the bigotry of the Church (Graham Greene's *The Living Room*).

If one simply considers the articles translated for the

[15] Ibid., p. 32.
[16] Ibid., p. 31.
[17] Ibid., pp. 42-43.

English-language edition,[18] *Mythologies* gives the somewhat misleading impression of a playful parody of the artifacts and events of mass culture, verging on complicity. What is excluded is a fairly substantial number of pieces in which Barthes reveals himself to be a skillful demystifier in the Marxist tradition. For example, his dissection of Elia Kazan's *On the Waterfront* shows how the naiveté of the Brando character becomes the point of view of the film and thus displaces our view of the source of corruption from the capitalists to the gangsters, and the solution of the problem from working-class revolt to Christianity. Barthes's inspiration in this article is Brecht, long an object of Barthes's admiration, who mastered the art of distancing the spectator from the naive hero without alienating sympathy for him. Barthes's articles on Poujadism are impressive "demystifications" of petit-bourgeois thought, which is motivated by illusory common-sense standards of tautology and calculation (of credit and debt), and which quickly settles all questions, dissolves all doubts, and closes up the world. There is a scorn, a moral severity in Barthes's manner in those articles, suggesting a confident possession of the truth. The presence of these articles would seem to justify Barthes's portentous demystifying claim in his long concluding essay that the petit-bourgeois spirit lies concealed in the myths. In phrases that echo Marx of *The Eighteenth Brumaire of Louis Bonaparte*, Barthes characterizes bourgeois ideology as an exercise in ex-nomination in which bourgeois reality is dissolved in a vocabulary that is universalistic. To reduce Barthes to Marx, however, is to miss the paradoxical outcome of Barthes's performance. He is less concerned to point a finger at the bourgeois demon lurking in the myths that it generates than he is in examining the process by

[18] See French edition of *Mythologies* (Paris: Editions du Seuil, 1957), particularly pp. 74-76, 96-98, and 205-212. The recently published *The Eiffel Tower and Other Mythologies*, trans. Richard Howard (New York: Hill & Wang, 1979) includes articles from the French edition of *Mythologies* excluded from the American edition.

which the very term bourgeois disappears in the mystification. Without fully knowing it, Barthes is a participant in the process of ex-nomination.

Though Barthes has not abandoned his claim to a leftist position, the reader is—or should be—uncomfortable with the ease with which Marxist and existentialist categories achieve substantiality in Barthes's discourse. Against the closed petit-bourgeois language of common-sense reason, Barthes proposes the subversive openness of dialectical reason, but the proposal is made in the space of short articles which close quickly and in which there is very little dialectical pressure (though often brilliant perception). In this connection we may recall Barthes's criticism of La Rochefoucauld's aphoristic method, which prematurely arrests the process of demystification. Of course, Barthes is never without a compensatory lucidity about his own inadequacies.

> An aphoristic tone hangs over this book (we, one, always). [The tone characterizes *S/Z* and *A Lover's Discourse* as well as *Roland Barthes by Roland Barthes*. It is characteristically Barthesian.] Now the maxim is compromised in an essentialist notion of human nature, it is linked to classical ideology: it is the most arrogant (often the stupidest) of the forms of language. Why then not reject it? The reason is, as always, emotive: I write maxims (or I sketch their movement) *in order to reassure myself*: when some disturbance arises, I attenuate it by confiding myself to a fixity which exceeds my powers.[19]

One is reminded here of the disarming tactic of myth: to justify oneself in the confession of a fault.

The myths that Barthes treats have indeed become universal. The fact that they originated in the mind of a corporate entrepreneur and are sponsored by the profit motive contributes little, if anything, to our sense of the life

[19] *Roland Barthes by Roland Barthes*, p. 179.

they have in the minds of the people. "It is . . . when a typist earning twenty pounds a month *recognizes herself* in the big wedding of the bourgeoisie that [Barthes declares] bourgeois ex-nomination achieves its full effect."[20] If the bourgeois wedding is a real possibility for the typist—as is jet travel—one nevertheless continues to question the quality of life incarnated by bourgeois marriage and jet travel. On what grounds do we demystify, on what basis do we criticize? And indeed, in an essay, "La Mythologie Aujourd'hui," written fourteen years after *Mythologies*, Barthes belatedly recognizes that the modern task is evaluation, not demystification. To be sure, Barthes attributes his perception to the changing times, not to a failure to perceive what was already the case in 1957 when he published *Mythologies*.

In *Roland Barthes*, he speaks of 1971 as the year in which the phrase " 'bourgeois ideology' had gone considerably sour and was beginning to 'fatigue.' "[21] I am suggesting that the problem is already apparent in *Mythologies*. If Barthes had not reached the point of emotional revulsion from Marxist cliché when he wrote *Mythologies*, "bourgeois ideology" was nevertheless extremely vulnerable even then as an explanatory term. So deep is the commitment to Marxist ideology in the French avant-garde intellectual, so lacking has he been in alternatives, that despite his lucidity in 1975, he must perform an act of ritual obeisance by saying: "Not that he [Barthes in 1971] denies this ideology its bourgeois stamp for a moment (quite the contrary: what else would it be? . . .)" How can Barthes avoid invoking the bourgeois in writing about the commodity world, that is, the world of contemporary myths? The cultural habit is so strong that the "evaporation of reality" that would follow from such an avoidance would be painful indeed.

The role of demystification vis-à-vis capitalism has always been marked by ambiguity. Marx understood capitalism

[20] *Mythologies* (American edition), p. 141.
[21] *Roland Barthes by Roland Barthes*, p. 89.

itself as a demystifying process in which the veil of illusion, which so effectively masked the economic realities of feudalism, is lifted in order to reveal the cash nexus that constitutes the social structure. At times Marx seems to view capitalism as the first society to propose an anti-idealist conception of itself. (Incidentally, the deliberate poverty of bourgeois idealization may be the cause of that peculiar phenomenon: bourgeois self-hatred.) At other times Marx stresses the mystifications of bourgeois society, its denial of its particularity in a universal ideology. The greatest of bourgeois slogans—liberty, equality, and fraternity—purports to speak for all men, but actually serves to mask a particular class interest. Even in the realm of production, the end result, the commodity, acquires in commodity fetishism the radiant features of transcendence, a view that conceals its source in human labor. Indeed, so strong is the impulse toward mystification that Marx ruefully remarks: "The recent scientific discovery that the products of labour, so far as they are values, are but material expressions of the human labour spent in their production, marks, indeed, an epoch in the history of the development of the human race, but, by no means dissipates the mist through which the social character of labour appears to us to be an objective character of the products themselves."

Commodities compensate for the religious disenchantments of the bourgeois world. They provide the experience of transcendence that religious relics used to provide in earlier times. If Marx hoped that it was only a matter of time before those mists were dissipated, he would surely have been disappointed. For as capitalism develops, its demystifying function weakens and its mystifications become more powerful and impressive. So powerful, in fact, that the ground reality that makes demystification possible appears to have been usurped or to have evaporated. Barthes's Cartesian inclination to discover emptiness seems justified by the increasing hegemony of capitalism. He himself suggests a reason for the difference between his situation and that of Marx. "It is possible that in Marx's day the pressure of culture on the proletariat was weaker than it is now; in the absence of 'mass communication,' there was as yet no 'mass culture.' "[22] Without the ground reality, Barthes's use of a Marxist method in the essay on myth is almost parodic ("almost" because, as I have shown, Barthes's assumptions preclude parody). Barthes tries to compensate for the empty prospect created by demystification. "Even here, in these mythologies, I have used trickery: finding it painful constantly to work on the evaporation of reality, I have started to make it excessively dense, and to discover in it a surprising compactness which I savoured with delight."[23]

Barthes is not the first critic to succumb to the temptations of the myths of mass culture. In *Tradition of the New* (1960) Harold Rosenberg found himself annoyed with "the mentality of those who keep handling the goods [of what he calls 'the cultural supermarket'] while denying any appetite for them."[24] And he singled out Dwight MacDonald for particular scorn. "MacDonald's taste for kitsch is largely negative, but it is genuine, at least genuine enough to yield him the time to become familiar with it. Modern art, however, revolts him; it gives him as much incentive to get to know it as would the gases in a condemned mine." Rosenberg was able to exempt himself from this condition because of his allegiance to high modern art. For Rosenberg as for Barthes, Marxism is a superannuated doctrine, which frees them both to engage in a kind of imaginative play with its categories. Like Marxism, however, modernism has now lost its power of resistance. In its present phase as exemplified by Barthes (a connoisseur and exponent of modernist literature), modernism, rather than resisting the myths of mass culture, has fully entered into them. I do

[22] *Image-Music-Text*, trans. Stephen Heath (New York: Hill & Wang, 1977), p. 210.

[23] *Mythologies*, p. 158.

[24] Harold Rosenberg, *Tradition of the New* (New York: McGraw-Hill, 1965), pp. 259-68.

not know whether Rosenberg has had his say about Barthes, but his strictures against the complicit critics of mass culture would seem to apply when he writes, "The people I am complaining about are the mass-art specialists, particularly the profound ones, those who cannot switch to Channel Four or roll over the corpse in a red chemise without beholding hidden patterns of the soul and society of contemporary man." But Barthes's serious and parodic treatment of contemporary myths would defy Rosenberg's judgment, compelling Rosenberg to articulate an adequate alternative, given the loss of authority of both Marxism and modernism.

The undermining of the critical authority of Marxism is epistemologically reinforced by semiotics. Marxism proves to be no more than another system of signs with no intrinsic claim to priority or even greater interest. Harold Rosenberg notes that "the moral [or psychological] issue of individual adherence [to the socialist movement] is irrelevant to Marx's conception of historical change."[25] A critic, not wishing to accept this limitation, might then engage in, let us say, a Freudian "demystification" of Marx or Marxism. On the other hand, there is no reason to believe that the "truth" or "reality" elicited by this kind of attention is ultimate truth. For example, a demystification of Lenin's hostility to the czar, which would understand it as an expression of an unresolved hatred of his father, simply places Lenin's revolutionary action in another semiotic system. It does not—or should not—reduce or explain away the action. What Barthesian semiotics does, against the method of demystification, is to insist that the two systems of explanation are *not* necessarily interpenetrable, so that one system need not unsettle the complacency of the other system. To see Lenin's revolutionism as a displacement of his Oedipal rivalry with his father may generate doubt about the disin-

[25] Rosenberg, *Act and the Actor: Making The Self* (New York: New American Library, 1970), p. 147.

terested justice of his revolutionism, but it will cast no doubt upon its objective necessity or correctness, unless psychological reality is shown to be prior to or determinative of political reality.

Mythologies is not Barthes's Marxist work, as some critics have taken it to be, but the work in which he enacts his abandonment of Marxism. Having relinquished Marxism as a basis for a demystifying criticism, Barthes finds himself in the painful negative state of exclusion. The only choice that he says exists for him is unsatisfactory: "either to posit a reality which is entirely permeable to history, and ideologize, or conversely, to posit a reality which is ultimately impenetrable, irreducible, and in this case, poeticize."[26] *Mythologies* concludes with a utopian yearning for "a reconciliation between reality and men, between description and explanation, between object and knowledge."

Barthes has not reconciled the divisions. Indeed, it is a real question whether the desire for reconciliation is anything more than a rhetorical flourish, a vestige of an older perspective that the very terms of Barthes's discourse has made impossible. If reality is empty or inchoate or a structure realized by another semiotic system, it is not clear that one can speak of reconciliation at all. What are the terms to be reconciled? If one assumes the ontological otherness of reality, all that one can say is that in the work that follows *Mythologies*, Barthes seems either to accept the divisions as insurmountable, or, which amounts to the same thing, to allow one of the terms of the division to devour the other term. The equivalent of the ex-nomination of the bourgeois occurs in the triumph of semiosis, the absorption of reality into that willful activity of language that Barthes calls *écriture*.

In one of his essays on Sade, in *Sade-Loyola-Fourier*, Barthes cheerfully acknowledges that the meaning (semiosis) dis-

[26] Barthes, *Mythologies*, p. 158.

torts what is represented (mimesis), and then proceeds to dismiss the mimetic aspect of Sade's work: "It is on the level of meaning, not of the referent, that we should read him."[27] The interest of Sade is in the system of words or linguistic units rather than in the admittedly monotonous cruelty of the action. Barthes's claim for Sade resembles a conservative exercise in the domestication of the text—which, of course, it is not intended to be.

Whether language and reality are cut apart from each other (the surgical image is Barthes's), or whether reality is simply absorbed into or distorted by language (Barthes is not consistent), the result is the same: reality never tests or constrains language. Sade's greatness lies in his virtuosic manipulation of a vast system of signs that he has created, not in "having celebrated crime, perversion, nor in having employed in this celebration a radical language."[28] Barthes finds support for his reading in Sade's plausible claim that "I have conceived all that can be conceived along that line, but I have certainly not done everything I have conceived and I shall certainly never do it."[29] And surely as Barthes notes "the complexity of the combinations, the partner's contortions, the potency of ejaculations, and the victims' endurance all surpass human nature: one would need several arms, several skins, the body of an acrobat, and the ability to achieve orgasm *ad infinitum*."[30] But the evident truth of this claim, so wittily and persuasively phrased, conceals a sleight of hand that is intended to disparage an interest in realism per se (of a Balzac or a Tolstoy, for example). "Why not test the realism of a work," Barthes asks, "by examining not the more or less exact way in which it reproduces reality, but on the contrary the way in which reality could or could not effectuate the novel's utterance?"

[27] Roland Barthes, *Sade-Fourier-Loyola* [1971], trans. Richard Miller, 1971 (New York: Hill & Wang, 1976), p. 37.

[28] Ibid., p. 126.

[29] Ibid., p. 137.

[30] Ibid., p. 136.

The question raised about Balzac and Tolstoy would receive a quite different answer from the one raised about Sade. But the more important point to make is that Barthes asks the question in a rhetorical manner, clearly interested in the way in which reality *cannot* effectuate the novel's utterance. What occupies Barthes is that aspect of a work, which is autonomous, irreducible, free of the constraints of reality, a word, incidentally, that Barthes tends to enclose in quotation marks.[31]

The capacity of language to realize or incarnate the inchoate experience is endlessly exemplified by Barthes's second essay on Sade. For example, the following passage on language and crime:

> Let us (if we can) imagine a society without language. Here is a man copulating with a woman, *a tergo*, and using in the act a bit of wheat paste. On this level, no perversion. Only by the progressive addition of some nouns does the crime gradually *develop*, grow in volume, in consistency, and attain the highest degree of transgression. The man is called the *father* of the woman he is possessing, who is described as being *married*; the amorous act is ignominiously termed *sodomy*; and the bit of bread bizarrely associated in this act becomes, under the noun *host*, a religious symbol whose flouting is sacrilege. Sade excels in *collecting* this pile of language: for him, the sentence has this function of founding crime: the syntax, refined by centuries of culture, becomes an *elegant* (in the sense we use the word in mathematics, a solution is elegant) art; it collects crime with exactitude and address: "To unite incest, adultery, sodomy, and sacrilege he buggers his married daughter with a host."[32]

[31] If one consults one's experience of the text, one must demur from Barthes's conviction that reality has been absorbed by the signifier. The essays on Sade have more power than the essays on Loyola and Fourier because the scandal of the referent informs the play of the discourse.

[32] *Sade-Fourier-Loyola*, pp. 156-57.

Elsewhere he speaks of writing that produces pornograms, which regulate "the exchange of Logos and Eros making it possible to speak of the erotic as a grammarian and of language as a pornographer." The pleasure of the text consists not in sadism, "its coarse (vulgar) content," but in the creative power of the text to *incorporate* the contents, to *collect* a pile of language and to refine it into an elegant art. In an essay "Proust and Names" Barthes speculates about the realistic basis of all writing, that is, realistic in the scholastic sense of the term, and he asks rhetorically whether it is possible to be a writer without believing that names incarnate essences; or in Saussurean terms, that signifiers incarnate signifieds. He speaks of a "natural relation between names and essences."[33] Barthes acknowledges that such a view goes contrary to Saussurean nominalism, which holds that signs are arbitrary. He comes perilously close to an organicist view of literature, so intense, so physical is his feeling for the life of words. On the other hand, the division between signifier and signified gives language its extraordinary freedom to multiply "meaning." Any attempt to enclose both terms in a totality or unity would destroy the freedom and richness that the division makes possible.

The liberation of the signifier from the signified is the correlative of the triumph of the pleasure principle over the reality principle. The signified, like the reality principle, represents the limiting conditions of existence. The signifier, like the pleasure principle, transgresses the limits of the signified. The transgressions that produce pleasure interrupt the binding, repressive continuities of reality. The liberated signifier enhances the power of language because of its capacity for multiple meaning. Not that the signifier is ever without its conditions or constraints, but the constraints themselves are variable. They are in fact necessary, like the friction that increases pleasure. The constraint itself

[33] "Proust and Names" in *New Critical Essays*, trans. Richard Howard (New York: Hill & Wang, 1980), pp. 67-68.

is invented by the liberated signifier, which creates the forms of experience.

And yet the specter of totality haunts Barthes's work, if only because it "represents" an inextinguishable need or appetite. The specter can be discerned not only in the pathos of his yearning for reconciliation (in *Mythologies*), it is to be found in the very terms of his account of the loss of authority that demystification has suffered. If it can no longer depend upon a substantial reality that survives the process, demystification becomes the agent of the evaporation of "reality" (which, because it has become illusory, must be enclosed in quotation marks). But Barthes, as we have already seen, is not satisfied by empty spaces. His animus against totality doesn't work in the direction of the minimal, the ascetic. Rather than empty space, he wants to create as much motion as he can within the space. Barthes's text has its own kind of fullness.

Barthes's "honesty" in acknowledging his trickery in *Mythologies* disarms any incipient irritation with his deceit in filling those spaces. It is not hard to forgive him his appetite for fullness. Barthes's disclosure of his own strategy, which always reveals a certain resentment against honesty itself as if it were a vestige of the bugbear nature (or the *natural*), is persistent. In *S/Z* (a book published a year before *Sade-Loyola-Fourier*) Barthes admits the duplicity involved in permitting the multivalent text that he is creating to overwhelm the classic text of *Sarrasine*. If Barthes does not wear duplicity as a flag, it nonetheless functions as a mark of his sophistication, which prohibits a genuine belief in the possibility (and the desirability) that the division he regretted in *Mythologies* can be overcome.

> A multivalent text can carry out its basic duplicity only if it subverts the opposition between true and false, if it fails to attribute quotations (even when seeking to discredit them) to explicit authorities, if it flouts all respect of origin, paternity, propriety, if it destroys the voice

> which could give the text its ("organic") unity, in short, if it coldly and fraudulently abolishes quotation marks which must, as we say, in all *honesty*, enclose a quotation and juridically distribute the ownership of the sentences to their respective proprietors, like subdivisions of a field. For multivalence (contradicted by irony) is a transgression of ownership. The wall of voices must be passed through to reach the writing: this latter eschews any designation of ownership and thus can never be *ironic*; or, at least, its irony is never certain (an uncertainty which marks several great texts: Sade, Fourier, Flaubert). Employed in behalf of a subject that puts its imaginary elements at the distance it pretends to take with regard to the language of others, thereby making itself even more securely a subject of the discourse, parody, or irony at work, is always *classic* language. What could a parody be that did not advertise itself as such? This is the problem facing modern writing: how breach the wall of utterance, the wall of origin, the wall of ownership?[34]

Barthes's need to *destroy, transgress, subvert, flout, abolish* in writing: words that evoke crime or revolution suggest that his affinity for Sade is reflected not only in Sade's virtuosity as a player with signifiers, but in the content (i.e., what is signified) as well. Though he plays with the idea of criminality, Barthes's view is not criminal in the sense that he wishes to destroy ownership itself (a concept that is constitutive of criminality). What he wants to "gain" is access to *writing*.

The experience of writing is perhaps given its clearest expression in *The Pleasure of the Text* through an analogy with sexual experience in its ecstasy and its suffering. In order to gain access to "writing," Barthes needs to destroy the "organic" unity of the text, which he locates in "voice" and in "the hermeneutic narrative." What Barthes tries to accomplish, most notably in *S/Z*, is an orgasmic demolition

[34] *S/Z*, pp. 44-45.

of the body of the text (the organic image as adversary is persistent): "the total body must revert to the dust of words, to the listing of details, to a monotonous inventory of parts, to crumbling; language undoes the body, returns it to the fetish."[35] (This gloss on a detail of *Sarrasine* is an emblem of Barthes's own performance in *S/Z*.) The disruptive method of *S/Z*, which breaks up the narrative, arresting its "flow" at every imaginable place, is the perfect instrument of this erotic strategy. And the paradoxical effect (which Barthes obviously desires) is to make *Sarrasine* "excessively dense," not unlike what he accomplishes in *Mythologies*. Barthes's selection of *Sarrasine* is itself a paradox, because while Balzac's narrative unfolds toward the horrid emptiness of the castrato, Barthes's analysis compensates for the emptiness. Writing becomes a compensation for the loss of substantial reality.

The manner of the demystifier remains, but its content, so to speak, has been dissolved. Demystification presupposes not only the existence of a substantial reality anterior and external to its expression, it also assumes the possible ideal transparency of language, so that reality or truth can always challenge the words that are supposed to express it.

The belief in the transparency of expression has always been a bête noire for Barthes, who disposed of its claims on ideological grounds in the early work *Writing Degree Zero* by attributing it to the classical period in which the bourgeoisie began its rise to power. On linguistic grounds, Barthes views clarity as an illusion, which simply ignores the hermetic self-enclosed character of all semiotic systems. (To my knowledge, he never tries to account for the function of this illusion, if illusion it is, as a basis for dispelling ideological distortion and euphemism, though he himself has often brilliantly exercised the function.) The failure of language to be perspicuous to reality is not an occasion for regret. For Barthes it is the obverse of the power, the pleas-

[35] Ibid., p. 113.

ure, and the freedom of the literary mode. Barthes's intense hostility to transparent writing can be understood psychologically as an expression of a residual commitment to mystery. In his insistence on the hermetic character of all semiotic systems, Barthes has provided an opening in language itself "for the unspoken depths of reality."

For all of his capacity for demystification, Barthes's temperament often goes counter to it.[36] To demystify is to be out of sympathy with the text. The demystifier invents a structure against the visible structure of the text. In the act of making his structure visible he may pass from the condition of impotence to the illusion of power. But it is an illusion based on the sense of exclusion and informed by resentment, as Barthes himself remarks:

> All socio-ideological analyses agree on the *deceptive* nature of literature (which deprives them of a certain pertinence): the work is finally always written by a socially disappointed or powerless group, beyond the battle, because of its historical, economic, political situation; literature is the expression of this disappointment. These analyses forget (which is only normal, since they are hermeneutics based on the exclusive search for the signified)

[36] Barthes does show a taste for demystification in his admiration for the anti-novels of Robbe-Grillet, which he admires because of their ambition to purify the object world of the falsifying depths of human signification (profundity, interiority, transcendence), though he makes the damaging admission in one of his essays on Robbe-Grillet that it is an error of Robbe-Grillet to believe that there is a reality in things antecedent and exterior to language and signification. Robbe-Grillet's claim or aspiration to innocence in representing the surfaces of things would seem to be even more vulnerable to the charge of mystification leveled against contemporary myths precisely because of its strenuous air of unpretentiousness. Despite the admission, Barthes does not exhibit the same impatience that he says he feels in *Mythologies* "at the sight of naturalness" with which Robbe-Grillet undresses reality, to alter Barthes's phrase. If zero-degree authenticity is impossible, isn't it a most insidious form of inauthenticity even to pursue it, since such a pursuit misleadingly implies its possibility?

> the formidable underside of writing. Bliss, which can erupt, across the centuries, out of certain texts that were nonetheless written to the glory of the dreariest, of the most sinister philosophy.[37]

If demystification originally and ideally represented an effort to restore the truth and integrity of things, it has become both a vision and a condition of alienation, a symptom of powerlessness and a vain attempt to compensate for it. The demystifier's unfulfillment becomes a kind of asceticism, a mark of spiritual superiority. Hedonist that he is, Barthes finds the spirituality of unfulfillment uncongenial.

The social expression of a fulfilled condition is aristocratic society in which values have an impressive physical incarnation: impenetrable, irreducible, and poetic in Barthes's sense. The aesthetic appearances of the aristocratic world have an ultimate reality that precludes the possibility of demystification. When Jane Austen evokes Pemberley estate (in *Pride and Prejudice*), she presents an unproblematic, unalienated set of values, immediately apprehendable in our visualization of the estate. In the depiction of Pemberley estate, nature and art are indissolubly wedded, each preserving its integrity without cost to the other, a condition that leaves nothing to be desired and gives no reason for demystification. In contrast to the fullness of aristocratic life associated with its relation to the land, demystification which exposes emptiness would seem to be linked to capitalism. As Balzac has shown and Barthes has noted, Parisian riches are founded on the emptiness of financial speculation.

For Roland Barthes, "criticism" is the creation of a verbal space, comparable to an aristocratic estate, in which one is provided with pleasures impossible in contemporary reality. Among those pleasures, Barthes somewhat furtively imports "charms (not values) of the bourgeois art of living"

[37] *The Pleasure of the Text*, trans. Richard Miller (New York: Hill & Wang, 1975), p. 39.

which, from the point of view of socialism or whatever we call the society that transcends bourgeois society, would be a kind of exoticism. The critical intelligence names and classifies the objects of the space, which it has created and rules like a god. It is as if the metaphor of the writer creating a world is literalized or substantiated. The body of the world enters the process of writing, so that writing becomes a physical presence equivalent to reality. This is Barthes's myth of *écriture*.

The bodily character of *écriture* has interesting political implications. Bodies are finite and individual, not infinite and universal. Each person's verbal space is sacrosanct, just as each person's body is inviolate. Barthes's value terms are *différence* and *pluriel*. He protests against the tyranny that one language tries to impose on another. Difference "dispenses with triumphs." The increasing inwardness of his work (*Roland Barthes by Roland Barthes* and *A Lover's Discourse*) has led Barthes to confessions of insecurity. His "liberalism" is not simply a concession to otherness. It proceeds from an unwillingness, based on insecurity, to overvalue his own *imaginaire de la solitude* (the image system of solitude). His Nietzschean perception of the will-to-power inherent in all languages leads him in an un-Nietzschean manner to resist its murderous innocence. It is the other Nietzsche, who has transcended the contentions of power, who provides an analogous image to Barthes's dream of happiness. Nietzsche's utopia is an anti-community of artists, each creating his own world of beauty and power, which he governs with absolute authority. Nietzsche remarks somewhere: "Hundreds of profound lonelinesses together form the city of Venice: this is its charm, a picture for the men of the future."[38] Barthes is always restoring or recreating new verbal "bodies," which (in opposition to the

[38] Quoted in Karl Jaspers, *Nietzsche: An Introduction to the Understanding of his Philosophical Activity*, trans. Charles F. Wallraft and Frederick J. Schurtz (Tucson: University of Arizona Press, 1965), p. 283.

appropriative language that he often uses) are conceived as inviolate. Barthes's anarchist utopia bypasses the necessity of making a revolution.

In *Roland Barthes* one is struck by a persistent suggestion, indeed an offering of, a psychogenic basis for Barthes's thought as he himself had earlier offered a psychoanalytic understanding of the work of Michelet and Racine. Referring to the intimidating authority of the *natural*, Barthes speaks ironically of "how natural it is, in France, to be Catholic, married, and properly accredited with the right degrees."[39] It is difficult to see how Barthes had suffered from being a Protestant or from his failure (resulting from illness) to receive an *agrégation* and a doctorate. But Barthes's homosexual preference was unquestionably a continuous source of anxiety as it was for Proust (his favorite writer), Gide, and is for Genet. It is, I would suspect, the origin of his persistent need to assert the sacrosanctity of his own *imaginaire de la solitude*. Barthes goes beyond the usual apologetics for homosexuality by deuniversaling it, insisting on the plural term "homosexualities." What Barthes can be said to achieve is a kind of imaginative onanism in which one need not defer to, indeed one need scarcely acknowledge, the other. Barthes's imaginative onanism undermines his respect for the existence of other bodies, other image systems of solitude; in the experience of reading and writing, the "other" tends to be absorbed into a single, though multifarious, consciousness. I am not so much proposing a psychoanalytic reduction, or should I say demystification, as I am proposing a correlative to what is "finally" a linguistic phenomenon.

One may summarize Barthesian hermeneutics as follows: Having vaporized the intrinsic structure or structures of the text, the critic has nothing left to interpret. He is now free to engage in an activity resembling but quite different from interpretation, that of inventing or reinventing the

[39] *Roland Barthes by Roland Barthes*, p. 131.

text. Roland Barthes succinctly characterizes this activity in an early essay "What is Criticism?"[40] According to Barthes, criticism is sanctioned neither by its empirical fidelity to the text ("its task is not to discover truths") nor by the authority of its motive or purpose ("the language each critic chooses to speak does not come down to him from Heaven"), but by its own internal validity, for which there are only two conditions: 1) the internal consistency of the discourse and 2) the saturation of criticism with the object of which it speaks. The power of an act of criticism resides in the richness of its detail and the willful elegance of its structure. Barthes's "scientific" model for criticism is mathematical (logical or tautological) rather than empirical. On this view, criticism appropriates the text (Barthes will call the appropriation theft) in order to fill the new structure created by the critic or reader. The relation of criticism to the imaginative work is comparable to the relation of work to reality. The literary work has separated itself from the "reality" that might have been its occasion and constituted a "world." Similarly, criticism creates its own structure, losing all representational function.

The Barthesian critic wills the dissolution of the text, so that he can gain the freedom to impose his own text. In particular, he wills the dissolution of intention, structure, teleology, and wholeness (terms that denote the plenitude of the text). And yet he cannot escape the occasions and resistances that the text offers. The fullness of the text and the terms that denote it reassert their presence.

"Interpretation" in this transvalued sense is constrained neither by the text nor by the institution (i.e., whatever the occasion for interpretation), but by the coherent (or sometimes not so coherent) subjectivity of the interpreter. Criticism becomes self-reflexive in an unprecedented way. "All criticism," Barthes remarks (in "What is Criticism?") "must include in its discourse . . . an implicit discussion of itself;

[40] See *Critical Essays*, p. 260.

for to rephrase a play of words by Claudel, criticism is knowledge of the other and *co-naissance,*" a pun on knowledge and birth of oneself in the world. Yet given the terms of Barthes's discourse, does self-knowledge, let alone knowledge of the other, have meaning? Self-knowledge implies the kind of understanding that may be precluded by Barthes's assumption of indeterminacy or emptiness. Self-reflexivity (the more accurate term) has the effect of generating an enclosed subjective space (what Barthes calls his *imaginaire de la solitude*). What occurs is a constant, unending self-interrogation, but since the self is indeterminate or a linguistic construct, language itself becomes the object of interrogation—or play rather than interrogation. In producing a "writerly" text, Barthes means to create a theoretically endless play of signifiers, which forever eludes ultimate meaning.

In reading a Barthes text are we playing with it as Barthes is playing, for example, with *Sarrasine* in *S/Z*, or are we interpreting it, determining its intention? I think we are of necessity doing the latter. We are, in Barthes's terms, readerly readers, not writerly readers of his own text. Indeed, we may ask: What would it mean to play with a Barthes text? It would mean continuing in the playful spirit of the text. Such a statement assumes the text's objective status. As playful readers we would be as respectful of the spirit of the text as any readerly interpreters. "Irresponsible" writerly readings may be relevant only to classic works, which need to be played with in order to become alive with desire. But writerly works conversely invite or even require a stabilizing readerly impulse, so that they become intelligible and communicate. The first experience of *S/Z* (or *Ulysses*) is unintelligibility; we therefore apply to the work a hermeneutic or proarietic code to determine its intention. What the distinction between the readerly and the writerly does not eliminate is intention. The writerly is as much an intentional structure as the readerly.

By denying the attribute of ownership (authority) to the

text, Barthes presumably liberates the text (imaginative and critical) from repressive hierarchical constraints. The text inhabits a democracy or, better, an anarchy. But we know how anarchies tend to attract autocratic types. It is a curious fact that contemporary critics who argue for the indeterminacy of the text often assert their own views with remarkable confidence, even arrogance. They dominate, if not own, the text. To deny ownership to the text is to remove the sign *no trespass*, which is to allow the trespasser to possess the text. If criticism is theft, then the critic finds himself in the curious state of ownership, though, one might add, a provisional ownership that Barthes, for one, might be ready to relinquish to the next reader.

Barthes's imaginative career might be understood as an ascesis which is a *via media* to a new plenitude, freed of the impurities and corruptions of the world. Barthes's ascesis is the recuperation of the ecstatic plenitude of language or literature, demystified and remystified by a new "hermeneutics." All the talk about the pleasure of the text is a testimony to the experience. The desire for plenitude may be inextinguishable, a desire that may continue to attach human beings, whatever resistance they may offer, to god terms. At the same time Barthes resists or interrupts the career of desire, because of what complete satisfaction (as exemplified by what Barthes calls classic literature) entails.

Barthes's "appropriation" of the text is provisional. He does not seek the ultimate satisfaction of possession. He wants the disintegrative pleasure of a provisional "mastery" of the text. No reading or experience can satisfy desire. Moreover, as we have seen, Barthes does not aim at the complete satisfaction of desire, the nineteenth-century project of totalization, which he repudiates as a monstrosity.

> Let us imagine (if we can) a woman covered with an endless garment, itself woven of everything said in the fashion magazine (*Systeme de la Mode*). This imagination, apparently methodical since it merely sets up an opera-

> tive notion of semantic analysis ("the endless text"), actually (secretly) aims at denouncing the monster of totality (totality as a monster). Totality at one and the same time inspires laughter and fear: like violence, is it not always *grotesque* (and then recuperable only in an aesthetics of Carnival)?[41]

Writing is desire satisfied (not to the point of satiety) and immediately renewed. The animus against the monster of totality goes some way toward "explaining" Barthes's changefulness as a writer, his refusal to be fixed in any particular position, his unwillingness to come to rest on firm ground. Barthesian plenitude is rather the richness of language as it manifests itself through *semiosis*: the activity of writing (*écriture*) by which language generates a superfluity of "meaning"—without beginning or end.

One needs a paradoxical language to describe the writing/reading process as Barthes conceives it. The writer-reader acquires "authority" at the same time that the authority of both text and self (object and subject) are being challenged. The discovery of the indeterminacy or emptiness of the text does not necessarily lead to despair because of an extraordinary self-confidence of the writer-reader. If the text is indeterminate or empty, what is the reader? Why doesn't he disappear together with the author? Barthes does not explicitly address the question. But perhaps there is an implicit answer in the unreified provisionality of the reader, who is no more than an ephemeral creature of desire.

[41] *Roland Barthes by Roland Barthes*, pp. 178-80.

4

READING WITH/OUT A TEXT

For Roland Barthes, the pleasure of the text is in the making of one's own text at the expense of the text of another. "Thus begins at the heart of the critical work, the dialogue of two histories and two subjectivities, the author's and the critic's. But this dialogue is egoistically shifted toward the present: criticism is not an homage to the truth of the past or to the truth of 'others'—it is a construction of the intelligibility of our own time."[1] In shamelessly confessing the egoism of the critical act, Barthes casts doubt upon the objective existence of "others." If he were consistent, he would also have enclosed the past within quotation marks. Barthes's motive is to make the "other" vulnerable and defenseless, so that he can appropriate it to his own purpose: he speaks of the critical act as theft. Interpretation in this transvalued sense is not obliged to represent the text, which is, rather, broken up so that it can fill the critic's subjectivity. The critic's text is always provisional, his relationship to the text of the other constantly changing. In declaring "the death of the author," Barthes eliminates interference from an author's intention. The critical reader's access to the text is immediate, dominant, and impermanent. The critic need be faithful only to his own changing, desiring subjectivity.

Barthes's nemesis is "Replete Literature," "the monster of totality," which makes the reader submissive to its meanings and freezes desire. For Barthes Replete Literature is

[1] Barthes, "What is Criticism," in *Critical Essays*, trans. Richard Howard (Evanston: Northwestern University Press, 1972), p. 260.

constituted by bourgeois stereotypes (Balzac's *Sarrasine*, the text of *S/Z* is an example). " 'Life' then, in the classic text [the replete and totalized text], becomes a nauseating mixture of common opinions, a smothering layer of received ideas."[2] Such a text extinguishes the reader's mobility and desire and therefore the possibility of pleasure.

More than any writer on either side of the Atlantic, Roland Barthes has brought the reader into the foreground of a critical discussion. It was he who first undermined and usurped the independent text. When we turn to American reader-oriented critics, Stanley Fish, for example, we encounter significant differences. Barthes's vocabulary, in the French manner, has a metaphysical resonance. Words like nature, history, and totality suggest that every reading is more than an engagement with a particular text: it is a sort of philosophical or political meditation for which the particular text is an occasion. Fish's sensibility, in the Anglo-American manner, is empirical. If Fish denies the independent integrity of the text (which the New Criticism asserted), he virtually never rises above the interpretive occasion that it offers, though he is continuously theoretical about the nature of texts. Barthes's *pleasure* in and of the text disappears into a veritable *industry* of reader-oriented criticism, a reflection of another obvious cultural difference—though there is more intellectual pleasure in Fish's interpretations than in most American reader-oriented criticism. Whereas for Barthes the text is broken up or emptied so that the imaginative writer-reader may construct his own estate (Barthes is a lord of *écriture*), for Fish and his fellow readers, the text is largely an opportunity for interpretations by an academic community bound together by shared assumptions. The difference is between a kind of individualism and a kind of collectivism: Barthes, the exponent of a mandarin subjectivity, Fish, the democratic advocate

[2] Roland Barthes, *S/Z*, trans. Richard Miller (New York: Hill & Wang, 1974), p. 206.

of plural interpretive communities; though, as we shall see, Fish's pluralism is somewhat illusory.

I want to focus critically on the work of Stanley Fish, because among American reader-oriented critics he has been in the vanguard as an abolitionist of the independent text and a foremost advocate of the interpretive community as the source of authority. Fish did not decide against the independent text because of the "monster of totality," but the "god terms" of presence, value, freedom etcetera are, if not explicitly addressed, implications of his work, especially when placed alongside the speculations of other writers. According to the introductory essay in *Is There a Text in This Class?* (his collection of theoretical essays), Fish's career is the momentum generated by his attempt to answer the question, "Is the reader or the text the source of meaning?"[3] Against the prevailing New Critical orthodoxy that the text was the source of meaning, Fish decided in favor of the reader. As he discovered in the course of reading and debate, however, the idea of a stable, meaningful text did not disappear with the privileging of the reader. Like Barthes, Fish in his thinking about texts has undergone continual change (an abiding value for both), and the change has been in the direction of emptying the text, denying it inherent structure, properties, and intention: it is the reader who comes to realize the text.

Fish's conception of the role of the reader has also undergone change. If the reader is still in a privileged position in relation to the text, he is no longer an isolated entity; he now suffers the constraints of an interpretive community. Properties, structure, and meaning inhere neither in the reader nor the text. It is the community that provides the constraints formerly attributed to the text. The effect of communalizing the reader is to avoid "the rankest sub-

[3] *Is There a Text in This Class? The Authority of Interpretive Communities* (Cambridge, Mass.: Harvard University Press, 1980), p. 1.

jectivism."[4] Fish apparently believes that a communal consciousness is not a subjective one. Having already eliminated objectivism, he believes that he has also eliminated subjectivism not only by communalizing the reader, but by creating a constitutive model in which it is impossible to divide subject from object.[5]

Nonetheless, the effect of the model is to deny the substantial otherness of the text and to absorb it into the consciousness of the communal reader. Fish objects to another model of reader response, which holds that "the work is a repository of properties and meanings (corresponding to the intention of the author) which then come into contact with a reader more or less conformable to them." Fish speaks of this as an "adversary model" in which the work opposes the reader, and he attributes to it a static view of the encounter between reader and work.[6] On this view (according to Fish), the reader confronts a work of fixed meanings with his own, possibly divergent, fixed views. What Fish proposes is a view of the work in which whatever resistance the text may offer to the reader is overcome by the activity of the reader. Fish transcends the dualism of

[4] Ibid., p. 11.

[5] In his reply to an earlier version of this essay, Fish rightly called me to account for misnaming his model as transactive, rather than constitutive. My mistake, however, did not essentially affect my argument as Fish claimed it did.

[6] Ibid., p. 375. Only a view that demands that the world conform to one's idea of it would regard the encounter between reader and work (the meanings of which do not conform to views held by the reader) as necessarily adversarial. Moreover, adversarial books (i.e., books that assault one's cherished beliefs and provoke resistance, which may or may not be overcome by the work) are among the most rewarding experiences we have of literature. Fish attributes to this "adversary model" a static view of the encounter between reader and work. Why the reader necessarily confronts a work of fixed meanings with fixed views on the adversary model, as Fish maintains, is never explained. I don't mean to suggest that my account fits Fish as a reader, but it does fit the *persona* who opposes the "adversary model."

subject and object by effectively affirming the activity of the subject and denying the reality of the object.

Of course, one can never completely escape objectivism; it is, among other things, a necessary condition of polemic. For instance, Fish believes that a true, or at least false, interpretation of the post-structuralist or Derridian view is possible when he characterizes one of his own essays in the following way: "This essay is an attempt to dissociate myself from a certain characterization (*actually a caricature*) of the post-structuralist or Derridian position"[7] [italics added]. Objectivism is entailed in distinguishing between Fish's position and that of Derrida, and between Derrida's position and caricatures of it. It is difficult to see how Fish's model would contribute to the making of these distinctions. His dissociation from the post-structuralist position, however, is revealing.

> In the caricature . . . of the post-structuralist or Derridian view the denial of objective texts and determinate meanings leads to a universe of absolute free play in which everything is indeterminate and undecidable. In the view I put forward, determinacy and decidability are always available, not, however, because of the constraints imposed by the language or the world—that is, by entities independent of context—but because of the constraints built into the context or contexts in which we find ourselves operating. Thus I pursue a double strategy in the manner indicated by my title "Normal Circumstances, Literal Language, Direct Speech Acts, the Ordinary, the Everyday, the Obvious, What Goes without Saying, and Other Special Cases." I want to argue for, not against, the normal, the ordinary, the literal, the straightforward and so on, but I want to argue for them as the products of contextual or interpretive circumstance and not as the property of an acontextual language or an independent world.[8]

[7] Ibid., p. 268.

[8] Ibid.

The abolition of the independent text is not intended to change the way we live or, more specifically, the way we read, but only to change our theoretical understanding of what happens when we read. The intended effect is so benign that nihilism, even skepticism, seem to be inappropriate terms to apply to Fish's view.

For Fish, the normal, the everyday, and the straightforward cannot be taken for granted. They are sustained by an act of interpretive will that is always subject to collapse. Thus Shakespeare's *Coriolanus* in Fish's view is an expression, both in its theme and its form, of the precariousness with which "the social bond" (in which the everyday and the normal occurs) is constituted. On his reading, *Coriolanus* is a speech act about speech acts, which constitute the social bond.[9] The play becomes an occasion for Fish to assert his

[9] Fish's interest in speech-act theory reflects his commitment to the constitutive character of utterance. Statements do not merely mirror or reflect; they constitute the only reality there is. "According to Searle, the rules governing the making of a request (and of any other illocutionary act) are not regulative, but constitutive: that is, they do not regulate an antecedently existing behavior but define the conditions under which that behavior can be said to occur." Ibid., p. 201. But then the intentional character of the speech act is a problem for Fish. According to John Searle, speech-act theory assumes the intentional character of "a noise or a mark on a piece of paper to be an instance of linguistic communication. . . . One of the things I must assume is that the noise or mark was produced by a being or beings more or less like myself and produced with certain kinds of intentions." *Speech Acts: An Essay in the Philosophy of Language* (Cambridge: Cambridge University Press, 1969), p. 16. Fish allows the making of such an assumption as part of his theory, but would stress that it is only an assumption, which cannot be verified by reference to the text itself. "Only an assumption" weakens the necessity of making the assumption. Perhaps the nature of the intention is inacccessible or not fully accessible to another mind, but the fact of intention as something independent of that other mind is not merely an assumption: it is an intrinsic condition of the speech act and therefore *must* be assumed. In his prefatory note to his essay "How To Do Things with Austin and Searle," Fish corrects the objectivism of his discussion of *Coriolanus* (his claim that the play *is* a speech act), a necessary correction only if one remains faithful to the dubious premise that intentions do not inhere in a text. *Is There a Text?* p. 200.

view that "in fact men break those bonds whenever they like."[10] Fish could have said that men *may* break the bonds. The difference between the two conclusions is the difference between a logical and a historical view of experience. If one examines the logical conditions of the speech act as Fish does (following John Searle and J. L. Austin), one can draw the conclusion that men are free to deconstitute the social bond when they like. In history, however, men do not "enjoy" such freedom. More often than not, they maintain the bonds, because the risk of social or political retribution makes them fearful, or because the bonds have been internalized and present a psychological barrier too great to overcome. One of the citizens in *Coriolanus* says as much: "We have power in ourselves to do it, but it is a power that we have no power to do" (II, iii). What Fish does not take into account in his concern with the *logic* of speech-act theory are the *historical* circumstances that make the breaking of bonds possible or not. In moments of social crisis (created by economic difficulties or war, for example), the social bonds may be weakened or possibly strengthened, but even then, the phrase "whenever they like" would be insensible of the constraints that exist for most men in any society. It is an ahistorical view that makes possible Fish's statement: "Institutions are no more than the (temporary) effects of speech act agreement, and they are therefore as fragile as the decision [how fragile is this decision?], always capable of being revoked, to abide by them."[11] "Temporary" and "fragile" (unmodified by a sense of how durable these qualities may be)—how temporary and fragile, for instance, is the division between East and West Germany?—underestimates the difficulty of unmaking institutions and institutional agreements. The absence of a historical perspective (which, as we shall see, is characteristic in Fish's theoretical work) has radically skeptical, if not nihilist, im-

[10] Fish, *Is There a Text?* p. 203.

[11] Ibid.

plications, which Fish does not pursue by disposition and preference.

Fish thinks that he gains all the determinacy and even stability that he needs from "interpretive communities," though, significantly, he does not tell us how these communities arise and gain authority. All he can tell us is that they exist. Jonathan Culler, another exponent of reader-oriented criticism, finds Fish wanting precisely at the point where he invokes interpretive communities. "The task of literary theory or poetics," Culler writes, "is to make explicit the procedures and conventions of reading, to offer a comprehensive theory of the ways in which we go about making sense of various texts. But here Fish's theoretical enterprise abruptly vanishes."[12] Such a theory would have to be, in part at least, a historical theory, which itself becomes a text or a series of texts as volatile as any other text. (Where the independence and stability of texts are concerned, Fish makes no distinction, indeed argues against distinctions, between kinds of text.) I suspect that Fish stops short of offering a comprehensive theory of interpretive community because he wishes to exempt it from the unstable and dependent status of texts. The interpretive community, in fact, is the one relatively stable idea in Fish's constantly changing universe of reading. As a tacitly felt experience, the interpretive community paradoxically achieves the authority of constraint that it might lose if it became the explicit object of interpretive reading. If it became the explicit object of interpretive reading, we might see that it is an assumption as vulnerable to skeptical investigation as the view that meaning inheres in the text.

In any event, the interpretive community seems to guarantee agreement between its members.

> But given the notion of interpretive communities, agreement more or less explained itself: members of the same

[12] *The Pursuit of Signs: Semiotics, Literature, Deconstruction* (Ithaca, N.Y.: Cornell University Press, 1980), p. 125.

> community will necessarily agree because they will see (and by seeing, make) everything in relation to that community's assumed purposes and goals; and conversely, members of different communities will disagree because from each of their respective positions the other "simply" cannot see what is obviously and inescapably there: This, then, is the explanation for the stability of interpretation among different readers (they belong to the same community). It also explains why there are disagreements and why they can be debated in a principled way; not because of a stability in texts but because of a stability in the makeup of interpretive communities and therefore in the opposing positions they made possible.[13]

Does this mean that people within the same interpretive community never disagree, or that agreement is possible only within the same interpretive community? I can imagine disagreement between persons who share the same assumed purposes that would not be resolved by our appeal to those purposes, the purposes themselves being subject to different interpretations. Readers, after all, are distinguished from one another not simply by their purposes and assumptions, but by differences in intelligence and temperament as well. I can also imagine agreement across the boundaries of different communities. Fish's model of community, to the extent that it can be construed from the passage above, suggests a tedious, even dangerous homogeneity and stability, belied, I might add, by the liveliness of his disagreements with members of his own interpretive community. As an interpreter of enormous skill and ingenuity, Fish presents himself as very much his own man in a community of diverse views.

Fish means to affirm the rightness, the inevitability of this view of the interpretive community when he writes: "Thus the act of recognizing literature is not constrained by something in the text, nor does it issue from an inde-

[13] Fish, *Is There a Text?* p. 15.

pendent and arbitrary will; rather it proceeds from a collective decision as to what will count as literature, a decision that will be in force only so long as a community of readers or believers continue to abide by it."[14] Fish does not explain why a collective decision is less arbitrary than a decision made by an independent will, though it is true that a decision that has the force of a collective will may have a less arbitrary *appearance*. The arbitrary basis of Fish's conception of the interpretive community (it is more than a matter of appearance) can be seen in the possibility of an indeterminate number of communities in which the most outlandish readings are possible. If each interpretive community is law-abiding, the universe of interpretive communities is anarchic. Fish speaks of the possibility of a *Pride and Prejudice* in which Mr. Collins is not seen as the object of irony and of a legitimate Eskimo reading of "A Rose for Emily."[15] Such readings are improbable, if not impossible, in the community that Fish inhabits (hence the confidence with which he affirms the normal, the everyday, the obvious), but Fish's theory (in which the text has no inherent structure) makes the outlandish always possible. There are no objective standards for discriminating among the various communities.

Both the rigid lawfulness of the interpretive community and the anarchy of the universe of readings exclude the freely choosing, value-making individual self. Interpretations tend to be lawfully homogeneous within the community because interpreters have no choice; there is no adjudication possible between communities because interpreters are not free to move independently between them, not free, that is, ever to transcend their community.

Without the space of value-making, the very idea of an interpretive community (even in its collective manifestation) seems arbitrary, a necessity in an argument perhaps,

[14] Ibid., p. 11.
[15] Ibid., pp. 342, 346-48.

but without legitimacy. We never learn from what the authority of the community derives. In order to do so, one would have to provide a historical perspective that would yield, if not a general theory of the origins of authority, examples of how particular communities became authoritative. A historical perspective does not in itself provide standards for discrimination, but it does enable an understanding of why certain views gain authority and others do not. It also provides a place for the author: his or her intention and situation.

By "author," I do not necessarily mean an agency or function separate from the text: I mean what the author has gotten into the text to form its structure and properties. Though Fish on occasion seems to admit the author into the interpretive community,[16] the implication of his argument is that the author has no real place in it. It is not simply that the reader can never be sure about the author's intention; it is that whatever the reader may believe that intention to be is dictated by the assumptions of the community. Of course, this does not mean that the text is not already a constituted interpretation of something. The distance between interpreter and what is being interpreted does not require the view that the text does not have an intrinsic structure. (It should be pointed out that, in Fish's view, the text produced by an interpretation is as uncertain in its "objective" meaning—indeed, it has no objective meaning—as the original text is to the first reader.) Fish seems to have converted the pragmatic difficulty, perhaps impossibility, of ascertaining and evaluating the author's intention into an epistemological denial of its objective ex-

[16] One circumstance in which an Eskimo reading of "A Rose for Emily" is possible "would be the discovery of a letter in which Faulkner confides that he has always believed himself to be an Eskimo changeling" (ibid., p. 346). A frivolous instance that shows, I think, that Fish does not take authorial intentions seriously. Moreover, a letter after or beside the fact of a story is the least persuasive example of authorial intention. As I have already remarked, what counts is what has gotten into the text.

istence. Simply to assume the existence of authorial intention is to require the effort to discover it; to dissolve the assumption is to eliminate a valuable constraint within the interpretive community.

Thus the typological reading of *Samson Agonistes* (a reading that assumes that the Old Testament anticipates the New) is for Fish simply one possible reading of the poem. "For some present-day readers Christ is 'in the text' of *Samson Agonistes*, for others he is not, and before the typological interpretation of the poem was introduced and developed by Michael Krouse in 1949, he was not 'in the text' for anyone."[17] If the question becomes one of evidence, the answer is that there is no objective way of establishing the presence of typology in the text. Fish is right to say that the absence of reference to Christ may be evidence of "Milton's intention to respect typological decorum."[18] But the ambiguous nature of the evidence does not justify Fish's conclusion that it is the interpreter or the interpretive community that establishes its presence or absence. The question of the presence of typology should be addressed not only to the text, but also to the context in which it was written. (Fish is interested in the *present* context of the reader.) Continual reference to the assumptions of present interpretive communities dissolves attention to the text of the other and to the truth of the past.

The idea of interpretive communities has been with us for a while. Michael Polanyi has characterized the tacit assumptions by which scientists circumscribe the ground on which scientific progress occurs.[19] In *The Structure of Scientific Revolutions*, Thomas Kuhn argued that the motives that establish a particular "paradigm" as authoritative within a field are not purely scientific.[20] An understanding of sci-

[17] Ibid., p. 216.

[18] Ibid., p. 273.

[19] See, in particular, Michael Polanyi, *Personal Knowledge* (Chicago: University of Chicago Press, 1960).

[20] (Chicago: University of Chicago Press, 1964.)

entific progress depends in part on a sociology of sciences. In his recent work, Frank Kermode appeals to an institutional (i.e., academic) consensus in establishing the freedoms and constraints of interpretation as well as the "canon" to be interpreted.[21] Yet the standards and commitments of the academy have been deeply affected by a pervasive skepticism. Kermode's own appeal to institutional standards is hardly untouched by this skepticism. In a review of Kermode's *The Genesis of Secrecy*, Michael Fischer remarks that "to the extent that institutional pressures invest interpretation with appearance of significance, they also encourage the suspicion that criticism is an end in itself and foster the free play that Kermode thinks they restrain."[22] I suspect that Kermode is trying to voice the need for restraint at the same time that he finds the seductions of free *skeptical* play hard to resist. Yet Fischer's point is an important one, because it calls attention to the problematic character of the idea of an interpretive community in a time when everything is under suspicion. Do agreements occur because of the existence of interpretive communities or despite their absence? It is impossible to answer the question unless we know more than we at present know about the character of such communities.

Kermode suggests what a consensus of genuine conviction and commitment is like when he notes the belief in Christianity that motivates the work of most biblical scholars, who defend the truth of the gospels against all challenges: "Few would undertake the ardors of the training held necessary for serious work in Biblical criticism without some such prior commitment." Fischer says, surprisingly, that "literary criticism is not all that different." For Matthew Arnold, it was "not all that different," because criticism in his understanding and practice was an effort both to dis-

[21] "The Institutional Control of Interpretation," *Salmagundi* 43 (Winter 1979), 72-86, and *The Genesis of Secrecy: On The Interpretation of Narrative* (Cambridge, Mass.: Harvard University Press, 1979).

[22] *Salmagundi* 46-47 (Fall 1980-Winter 1981), 250-51.

cover spiritual values in secular literature and to rescue them from the dogmatizing and literalizing theological mind. But no such purpose determines the contemporary institutional study of literature. It is touching, but puzzling, that Fish should speak of "the bedrock of belief" that underlies the interpretive community.[23] This is the language of conviction singularly lacking in most interpretive communities today.

The interpretive community that sustains biblical scholarship depends upon a belief in the *presence* of the biblical text. Whether the presence is that of a divine voice or of an inspired human one is less important than the view that the text inherently contains something of utmost importance. Such a view makes it possible for the text to provide constraints to the interpretive community in addition to those provided by the social history of the community. I would guess that there is a correlation between, on the one hand, the confidence that the members of any interpretive community have in the validity and value of their interpretations and in the authority of the community and, on the other, the belief that what they read has an independent reality.

Of course, Fish can assimilate the belief in the presence of the text to his theory of interpretive communities. He would have to characterize the community of biblical scholars as naive in failing to recognize that its conviction rests on the false assumption that the text has presence. Yet what Fish's demystifying sophistication (assuming for the sake of argument that it is a true demystification) cannot account for is the consensus of genuine conviction and commitment of biblical scholars. Fish says that the truth of interpretation is ultimately a matter of its persuasiveness, which he equates with politics.[24] Why should we be *persuaded* by an interpretation (as distinguished from being impressed by its inge-

[23] Fish, *Is There a Text?* p. 136.
[24] Ibid., p. 16.

nuity) if we don't believe that it corresponds—or better, responds—to a presence in the text? Whether such a view is naive or not, that is what it means to be persuaded. One is not persuaded simply because one belongs to the same interpretive community. "The interpretive community" (as Fish conceives it) is as intrinsically vacuous as any text. Though it may be a requirement of the argument, it does not explain the agreements and stabilities of interpretation. The empty formalism of Fish's interpretive community corresponds to the unstable and dependent text just as the inspired commitment of the biblical community of scholars reflects or is reflected in the (divine) presence of the biblical text.

The belief that a text has inherent properties need not severely curtail the freedom of the critical reader. It does not preclude the indeterminacy of texts. In fact, there is a degree of indeterminacy in all texts that varies according to the suggestiveness of the text. Indeterminacy is a perpetual provocation to readers to interpret texts again and again. There are even moments when a reader may be torn between possible interpretations and unable to decide between them. Indeterminacy is not necessarily a function of the absence of intrinsic structure or the substantial otherness of the text. It is in part what spills over the boundaries of the text (the implications beyond what is explicit) and in part the inherent incapacity of one mind (that of the reader) to make a perfect adjustment to the mind of another (as represented by the text). It is a false logic to infer a reader whose mind is tabula rasa, as Jonathan Culler does in his approval of what he calls "Fish's theoretical reorientation," from the idea "that the poem is some kind of autonomous object which contains its meaning as an inherent property."[25] The reader need not suspend his subjective disposition in reading a poem that is filled with meaning. Culler's statement is equivalent to a view that, in a rela-

[25] Culler, *The Pursuit of Signs*, p. 21.

tionship between two people, one has to be dead for the other to be alive.

Wolfgang Iser puts the case well for an indeterminacy that proceeds from the substantial otherness of the text. In speaking of a novel by Ivy Compton Burnett, Iser asks us to "bear in mind the fact that the speakers are not aware of the welter of the implications they bring about and can themselves only reveal these implications to a limited extent."[26] Presumably, the narrative consciousness has a fuller understanding of the welter of implications than the characters themselves. But it is also true that the narrative consciousness in fiction does not fully know itself, hence the need for the critical reader. In turn, the critical reader may not be fully aware of the welter of implications of his or her own discourse, hence the need for the critics of critics. Though "the welter of implication" complicates, it does not dissolve the substantial otherness of a text.

The welter of implications may never be possessed by any particular reader, who appropriates a work according to his disposition and purposes. But he is not given license to distort at will so long as the text has its inherent structures and intentions. An empty text is indeterminate only in the sense that there is nothing to determine in an objective sense. It is the reader who forms and determines the interpretation, or rather, forms and determines the text itself. "Indeterminacy" should be reserved for the full or structured, not the empty, text. I can illustrate degrees or kinds of appropriation (on this side of distortion) by contrasting two readings of Abraham's intended sacrifice of Isaac, one by Erich Auerbach and the other by Søren Kierkegaard.

In the opening chapter of *Mimesis*, Auerbach distinguishes between the biblical and the Homeric methods of the representation of reality as a basis for subsequent inter-

[26] *The Implied Reader: Patterns of Communication in Prose Literature from Bunyan to Beckett* (Baltimore: The Johns Hopkins University Press, 1974), p. 248.

pretation of Western representations of reality. The methodological interest of Auerbach's reading (genuine as it is) serves what might be called a pious view of the biblical story.

> A journey is made, because God has designated the place where the sacrifice is to be performed; but we are told nothing about the journey except that it took three days, and even that we are told in a mysterious way: Abraham and his followers rose "early in the morning" and "went unto" the place of which God had told him; on the third day he lifted up his eyes and saw the place from afar. That gesture is the only gesture, is indeed the only occurrence during the whole journey, of which we are told; and though its motivation lies in the fact that the place is elevated, its uniqueness still heightens the impression that the journey took place through a vacuum; it is as if, while he traveled on, Abraham had looked neither to the right nor to the left, had suppressed any sign of life in his followers and himself save only their footfalls.[27]

Auerbach insists on the necessity for the empty spaces between the spare facts of the story. To fill the spaces with descriptions of landscape or with psychological motivation would divert the reader from the goal of Abraham's journey: the reencounter with God on Mount Moriah. Auerbach's piety, perhaps an expression of the link between his secular humanism and an older religious humanism, is to make the text speak through him. That is, he tries to make the intention of the tale as transparent as possible. His reading is—or purports to be—mimetic, and therefore a pious, act. It is an objective account in the sense that it is faithful to the facts of the story. But it is not an exhaustive account, since it avoids pursuing possibilities that the spareness of the tale implies through its suppressions. For example, when Auerbach says that "we are told nothing about the journey except that it took three days, and even that

[27] *Mimesis: The Representation of Reality in Western Literature* (Princeton: Princeton University Press, 1968), pp. 9-10.

we are told in a mysterious way," the invitation to speculate about what transpired during the journey is suppressed. But the very fact that it is perceived or felt as a suppression means that there is something there or something experienced as absent.

It is this suppressed area that is illuminated by Kierkegaard in *Fear and Trembling*, the effect of which is to appropriate and subjectivize the story in two senses. We enter into the minds of the characters as we do not in the original story, and there is a sense in which the original story is rewritten or filled in by Kierkegaard, who is telling the story of his own consciousness of God and the problem of evil (or rather that of his ethico-rationalist persona, Johannes de Silentio).[28]

> Then Abraham lifted up the boy, he walked with him by his side, and his talk was full of comfort and exhortation. But Issac would not understand him. He climbed Mount Moriah, but Isaac understood him not. Then for an instant he turned away from him, and when Isaac again saw Abraham's face it was changed, his glance was wild, his form was horror. He seized Isaac by the throat, threw him to the ground, and said, "Stupid boy, . . . dost thou suppose that this is God's bidding? No, it is my desire." Then Isaac trembled and cried out in his terror, "O God in heaven, have compassion upon me. . . . I have no father upon earth, be Thou my father!" But Abraham in a low voice said to himself, "O Lord in heaven, I thank Thee. After all, it is better for him to believe that I am a monster, rather than that he should lose faith in Thee."[29]

The effect of Kierkegaard's retelling is to displace attention from the goal to the motive. Though Kierkegaard

[28] I am grateful to Phillip A. Stambovsky for reminding me that the story is retold by Johannes de Silentio, an ethical rationalist against whom Kierkegaard will affirm his faith.

[29] Trans. Walter Lowrie (Princeton: Princeton University Press, 1968), p. 27.

remains on this side of blasphemy, he cannot avoid provoking the blasphemous sentiment that the very enterprise of responding to the empty spaces entails. It is difficult to resist the speculation that if Isaac believes that his father is a monster, it is because of a manipulated displacement from the real monstrous object: God himself. Kierkegaard fills the spaces between the facts in order to satisfy a modern doubt about Abraham's motivation. In this process of justifying Abraham's faith, he leaves a shadow on the divine conditions of that faith, which the modern reader may or may not choose to ignore. Yet for Kierkegaard, the text remains sacred; no fact is violated. If the surface of the story is insufficient, it must be enhanced, not penetrated to a darker and contradictory underlying truth.

The model implied in these instances is a transactive model, in which the text is objectively present and in which the individuality of the interpreter, whatever he shares with his interpretive community, is irreducible. It assumes vitality and activity on both sides of the transaction.

The paradox of reader-oriented criticism as Fish and others conceive it is that it weakens the authority of the reader as well as the text. (In Fish's case, the reader—not necessarily Fish in practice—becomes the instrument of communal determinism.) With the emptying of the text, the reader no longer has a text to experience. If he can be said to experience anything in the act of reading, it is the activity of his own mind. But it is only by stretching the meaning of experience that we can speak of reading, thus understood, as experience of something beyond itself. Reading becomes an exercise in theory or theorizing, a reflection upon the conditions of reading. The skeptic does not simply read; he tells us what happens when he reads, or when we read. The New Reader may even tell us that it is impossible to read. This last is the claim of deconstruction, the most radical of skepticisms about the text.

A subjectivity that presupposes the emptiness of the text (or the world) can never remain secure even in its subjectivity. As the subjectivity is objectivized and scrutinized, it too becomes an object of doubt. Are we to trust the experiencing "I"? Do we know what constitutes the "I"? Are we even sure it exists? The deconstructionists, who pride themselves on the superior rigor of their skepticism, devote themselves to destabilizing all the terms of *their* understanding, including their own rhetorical tropes. The relation between reader and text can be understood as a relation between the "I" and the world, if the text is conceived as embodying a meaning that refers to the world. And if the world and text conspire to be radically indeterminate or empty of meaning, then reading itself (the activity performed by the "I") becomes the object of interpretation and uncertainty. What survives the skepticism is the play of the skeptical will. Even as the skeptic doubts his own experience, the will asserts itself either in the form of an ingenious or creative reader, inventing doubtful "interpretive structures," or in the form of a deconstructive reader, dissolving structures, including the structure of interpretive community. It may be an expression of "the intelligibility of our time" that even the idea of an interpretive community (ostensibly an antidote to subjectivism) can exclude "the truth of the past" and "the truth of 'others.' "

The "monster of totality" is not a presence in the work of Anglo-American critics like Fish, so they are not possessed by the desire to destroy it. But consciously or unconsciously, every serious reader of literature participates in a process of secularization (of which the totalizing ambition of the nineteenth century is a version). The disappearance of the objective text is a consequence of secularization that has its origins in the Enlightenment. Before the Enlightenment, one may have doubted the authenticity of this or that biblical text, but the existence of an authentic biblical text was assumed, and authenticity meant derivation from divinity. God had spoken through the mediation of inspired human voices in the stories of the Bible. Much of the energy of intellectual life before the Enlightenment was devoted to the right understanding of the Word, the Text of texts. No existence was as substantial as that of the holy text.

The traditional conception of the indeterminancy of the text derives from the belief that the text is divinely inspired. Indeterminancy is a function of the infinite mind of God, to which the finite mind of every reader is inadequate. Behind our secular interpretations of secular works are centuries of biblical exegesis. Interpreters may differ about what or how much we may know of a text, but interpretation (again in the traditional sense) regards the text with the respect and care—if not exactly with the reverence—one reserves for sacred objects. Very few, if any, contemporary secular interpreters are prepared to accept the religious aura that Arnold conferred on poetry, but something of Arnold's habit of mind has persisted in the way close readers have talked about poems and poetry.

The aura of the literary work is the result of a saving secularization that tries to disengage spiritual (i.e., symbolic) meaning from the dogmatism of literal belief. The claim for the literary work becomes excessive in the wholesale transfer of spiritual significance from religion to literature. If the work or text is drained of its spiritual significance, a danger if the spiritual assertion loses its dogmatic authority, then there may be no need to value the text. Certainly, piety before the text (biblical or secular) becomes unnecessary. The next step is to deny the existence of the text. Since, however, the habits of reading and interpretation persist, the text is displaced from a world or space external to consciousness to the consciousness of the reader. Reading makes or unmakes the text. What survives of the older religious tradition in reader-oriented criticism is the Talmudic habit of paying an inordinate amount of attention to every mark on the page—not in deference to the sacredness of the text, but in the desire to exhibit one's interpretive skill.

In responding to an earlier version of this essay, Fish resolved all my doubts about the character of the interpretive community and the members that compose it. In using the phrase "suffers the constraints, . . . Goodheart imagines that I imagine a self *in need* of constraints, whereas in my account the self is a *structure* of constraints, in that its very possibilities—of action, interpretation and perception—are defined by the ways of thinking with which it has been furnished by a culture."[30] Fish misunderstands the intention of my phrase. I don't mean to imply that in Fish's current view the reader is ever outside that community. I mean, as the context of my statement should make clear, that in the development of Fish's argument the reader was once an isolated entity and now suffers the constraints of an interpretive community. But this is a quibbling matter compared with the matter on which we apparently agree: that for Fish the self (it hardly needs to be qualified as interpretive) is a predetermined structure of constraints without the freedom to deliberate effectively upon and to choose its assumptions and purposes.

Even if one were to grant that the self is a completely socialized or communalized structure (a reasonable, but not indisputable, supposition), it does not necessarily follow that the community produces homogenized products. Certainly not if the society or community is *not* totalitarian. In democratic society a community is a plurality of structures, that is, of differences and oppositions. A person may have internalized one combination of structures or another. He

[30] See *Daedalus* 112 (Winter 1983), 233. Though Fish has served as my example of radical subjectivism in reader-oriented criticism, he is by no means alone in his impulse to vaporize text and object. For example, David Bleich remarks that "Michaelangelo's *Moses* is no longer a block of stone in the shape of a seated man, but is a symbolic representation of something." *Subjective Criticism* (Baltimore: The Johns Hopkins University Press, 1978), p. 98. But why must it be either/or? A response to the sculpture that does not take into consideration its palpable properties (hardness, texture, shape) is clearly deficient not only in sensuous or aesthetic imagaination, but in its sensitivity to its symbolic aspect.

may be able to choose among the available structures, the configurations of which may change. And, indeed, if structures change, then who can say that the individual choosing self has not played a role in the change?

In disarming his critics, who have accused him of radical skepticism and "rank subjectivity,"[31] Fish asserts a model of the self that has lost a most valuable freedom: to decide the direction of its interests and understandings. It is, of course, possible that no such freedom exists, but since Fish has neither proved the existence of the self as a structure of constraints (in fact, it remains in his work a purely formal idea without psychological, moral, social, or historical substance), nor disproved the possibility of self-determination even should one grant the presence of restraints within the self, what remains of interest is Fish's choice to affirm a radically deterministic model of self and community. Out of the destructured and destabilized self, a new structuralism has in effect arisen. All interpreters are mere instruments of a community, whose values are so fixed (and beyond anyone's making) in communal consciousness as virtually to lose the name of values.

[31] The charge is not altogether without truth, for it applies, as I show, to the "universe of interpretive communities," if not to any particular community.

5

DISCOURSE WITHOUT FOUNDATION

In its heroic beginnings, secularization was an attempt to rescue the substance of religious truth from a moribund dogmatism that literalized god terms. To conceive of God, virtue, salvation, blessedness as symbolic terms was not to diminish the reality of the religious quest but to heighten it. In *Sartor Resartus*, Carlyle understood the process of secularization (the word is not his) as a process of rescue: "For it is man's nature to change his Dialect from century to century; he cannot help it though he would. The authentic *Church-Catechism* of our present century has not yet fallen into my hands: meanwhile, for my own private behoof, I attempt to elucidate the matter so." Carlyle never found that new dialect, but he was able to invest the old god terms with new associations.

In attempting to make all supernatural values worldly, secularization generates an atmosphere of equivocation in which the dominant term is constantly shifting. Religious vocabulary becomes metaphorical for psychological experience, but the inversion is unstable, because psychological or social experience is perceived at the same time as having a religious dimension. When Teufelsdröckh (the hero of *Sartor Resartus*) achieves the Everlasting Yea he finds not Happiness (a Utilitarian snare!) but blessedness, a spiritual state of being that equivocates between a religious experience and a psychological one. Teufelsdrockh is cured and saved. Though healing and salvation are virtually coextensive terms in orthodox Christian discourse, salvation is the dominant term. In the early phase of secularization there is no dominant term or the dominant term constantly shifts. The secularizing "progress" from religion to metaphysics and metaphor (the quintessential expression of language) leads to an increased interest in the nature of language generally. This interest may unfold in different directions.

In order to preserve religious and poetic values, one may try to demonstrate and affirm the constitutive powers of language. In Chapter 2, I cited Ransom's insistence that "the miraculism which produces the humblest conceit is the same miraculism which supplies to religions their substantive content." Of course, such a view may be regarded as sheer mystification; if it is "the poet and nobody else who gives to the God a nature," then the God is no more than a human fiction. The invitation to demystification is irresistible.

Yet this is by no means an easy task. We have the impressive testimony of Pierre Proudhon. However hard he tried, he could not cast out god terms from his materialistic understanding of the world.

> I am forced to proceed as a materialist, that is to say, by observations and experience, and to conclude in the language of a believer, because there exists no other; not knowing whether my formulas, theological despite myself, ought to be taken as literal or as figurative. . . . We are full of the Divinity, *Jovis omni plena*; our movements, our traditions, our laws, our languages, and our sciences—all are infected with this indelible superstition, outside of which we are not able either to speak or act, and without which we simply do not think.[1]

Though proceeding from motives quite different from Proudhon's materialist motive, deconstructionists like Jacques Derrida and Paul de Man have taken on Proudhon's task with an even more acute and sophisticated awareness of

[1] Quoted in M. H. Abrams, *Natural Supernaturalism* (New York: W. W. Norton, 1971), p. 66.

the difficulties. Like Proudhon, contemporary deconstructionists acknowledge the strength of the god terms they deconstruct.

The claim that metaphor, the principal god term of literary theology, is truth can be traced back to what Jacques Derrida calls "the great immobile chain of Aristotelian ontology, with its theory of the analogy of being, its logic, its epistemology, and more precisely its poetics and its rhetoric."[2] For Aristotle, metaphor is "an effect of *mimesis* and *homoiosis*, the manifestation of analogy."[3] It is this view that Derrida proceeds to deconstruct in his remarkable essay "White Mythology."

In order to do so, Derrida first establishes the metaphorical matrix of philosophy. "Metaphor seems to involve the usage of philosophical language in its entirety, nothing less than the usage of so-called natural language *in* philosophical discourse, that is, the usage of natural language as philosophical language."[4] Behind this formulation is a tradition of thought from Nietzsche to Heidegger. Derrida cites this passage from Nietzsche.

> What then is truth? A mobile army of metaphors, metonymics, anthropomorphisms: in short, a sum of human relations which become poetically and rhetorically intensified, metamorphosed, adorned, and after long usage, seem to a nation fixed, canonic, and binding; truths are illusions of which one has forgotten that they are illusions, worn out metaphors which have become powerless to affect the senses, coins which have their obverse *effaced* and now are no longer of account as coins but merely as metal.[5]

[2] Jacques Derrida, *Margins of Philosophy*, trans. Alan Bass (Chicago: University of Chicago Press, 1982), p. 236.

[3] Ibid., p. 238.

[4] Ibid., p. 209.

[5] Quoted in ibid., p. 217.

Metaphor is not only pervasive, it is the source of illusion, not truth—or rather the source of the illusion of truth.

The deconstruction of metaphor depends upon a perception that the "energy of metaphoric operation supposes . . . that the resemblance [between the metaphor and the term to which it is being compared] is not an identity [as Aristotle supposed]."[6] Derrida speaks of this perception as a dividend of pleasure, which enables him and us to see metaphor as a disseminating rather than unifying trope. And indeed, in order to avoid the threat of incoherence that metaphor always poses, philosophers have preferred "to choose the most worn out words from natural language."[7] Derrida cites Anatole France's *The Garden of Epicurus* in order to show how widespread this view is: "philosophers go out of their way to choose for polishing such words as come to them a bit obliterated already. In this way, they save themselves a good half of the labor. Sometimes they are luckier still and put their hands on words which, by long and universal use, have lost from time immemorial all trace whatever of an effigy."

Of course, philosophical discourse—or for that matter any discourse—cannot avoid the threat of metaphor, since so-called literal meaning is illusory: it is metaphor gone inert and dead and therefore unnoticed. The task of deconstruction, Derrida's task, is to recover the metaphoricity of thought both as a challenge to philosophy's claim to logical rigor and precise reference and as a revelation of the actual movement of thought.

> Metaphor . . . is determined by philosophy as a provisional loss of meaning, an economy of the proper without irreparable damage, a certainly inevitable detour, but also a history with its sights set on, and within the horizon of, the circular reappropriation of literal, proper meaning. This is why the philosophical evaluation of metaphor

[6] Ibid., p. 239.

[7] Ibid., p. 211.

> has always been ambiguous: metaphor is dangerous and foreign as concerns *intuition* (vision or contact), concept (the grasping or proper presence of the signified), and consciousness (proximity or self-presence); but it is in complicity with what it endangers, is necessary to it in the extent to which the de-tour is a re-turn by the function of resemblance (*mimesis* or *homoiosis*) under the law of the same.[8]

Derrida does not deny the law of the same, but in his perspective of the differential play of tropes, philosophy remains incorrigibly equivocal in its meanings. It is the detour rather than the re-turn that characterizes philosophical writing in the deconstructive view. One feels an ambivalence in Derrida's deconstructions, which, on the one hand, demystify philosophy's truth claims and, on the other, enter sympathetically into the metaphoric movement of thought itself, thereby revealing its "poetic" character. However ambivalent he may be, Derrida's essentially philosophical perspective erodes the distinction between literal meaning and figurative expression or between dead and living metaphor. As a consequence, such a view has none of the literary critic's interest in discriminating between the degrees of success a metaphor achieves or fails to achieve in discourse.

There is none of Derrida's ambivalence in Paul de Man's deconstruction of metaphor in literature. Rigorously ascetic in his readings, de Man almost scornfully resists the seductive claims of metaphor. In his recent book, *Allegories of Reading*, he exposes the activity of metaphor in a reading of a passage in *Swann's Way*, in which Marcel recalls a childhood experience:

> I had stretched out on my bed, with a book, in my room which sheltered, tremblingly, its transparent and fragile coolness from the afternoon sun, behind the al-

[8] Ibid., p. 270.

> most closed blinds through which a glimmer of daylight had nevertheless managed to push its yellow wings, remaining motionless between the wood and the glass, in a corner, poised like a butterfly. It was hardly light enough to read, and the sensation of the light's splendor was given me only by the noise of Camus . . . hammering dusty crates; resounding in the sonorous atmosphere that is peculiar to hot weather, they seemed to spark off scarlet stars; and also by the flies executing their little concert, the chamber music of summer: evocative not in the manner of a human tune that, heard perchance during the summer, afterwards reminds you of it but connected to summer by a more necessary link: born from beautiful days, resurrecting only when they return, containing some of their essence, it does not only awaken their image to our memory; it guarantees their return, their actual, persistent, unmediated presence.
>
> The dark coolness of my room related to the full sunlight of the street as the shadow relates to the ray of light, that is to say it was just as luminous and it gave my imagination the total spectacle of the summer, whereas my senses, if I had been on a walk, could only have enjoyed it by fragments; it matched my repose which (thanks to the adventures told by my book and stirring my tranquility) supported, like the quiet of a motionless hand in the middle of a running brook the shock and the motion of a torrent of activity.

"The passage" de Man asserts, "is *about* the aesthetic superiority of metaphor over metonymy."[9] Proust prefers the essential or necessary sensations of summer (hammering dusty crates, sparking scarlet stars, flies executing chamber music) to the accidental and contingent human tune "heard perchance during he summer," for the effect of metaphor is to produce "the total experience of summer" within the

[9] Paul de Man, *Allegories of Reading* (New Haven: Yale University Press, 1979), p. 14.

inner space of imagination that would be denied to him if he were outside in the natural world ("whereas my senses, if I had been on a walk, could only have enjoyed it by fragments").

But the text, according to de Man, does not practice what it preaches, since it does not show how the sensations that Marcel prefers are more essential than the accidental sensation of a tune heard by chance. Why are the several sensations that Marcel cherishes "connected to summer by a more necessary link" than the heard tune? De Man concedes that "the narrator is able to assert without seeming preposterous, that by staying and reading in his room Marcel's imagination finds access to 'the total spectacle of summer,' including the attractions of direct physical action, and that he possesses it much more effectively than if he had been actually present in an outside world that he then could have known by bits and pieces."[10] The passage is persuasive and the wonder is why this is so. De Man remarks: "There seems no limit to what tropes can get away with."

What de Man proceeds to argue is that "the assertion of the mastery of metaphor over metonymy owes its persuasive power to the use of metonymic structures."[11] According to de Man, Proust's persuasiveness depends upon devious and arbitrary exchanges of qualities (virtually a definition of metonymy) in which logically incompatible qualities are made compatible—as, for example, in the final sentence of the passage in which "the cool repose of the hand is made compatible with the heat of action."

> This transfer occurs, still within the space of a single sentence, when it is said that repose supports a 'torrent d'activité.' In French the expression is not—or is no longer—a metaphor but is a cliché, a dead or sleeping metaphor which has lost its literal connotations (in this case, the connotations associated with the 'torrent') and

[10] Ibid., p. 60.
[11] Ibid., p. 15.

> has only kept a proper meaning. 'Torrent d'activité' properly signifies a lot of activity, the quantity of activity likely to agitate someone to the point of making him feel hot. The proper meaning converges with the connotation supplied, on the level of the signifier, by the 'torride' ('hot') that one can choose to hear in 'torrent.' Heat is therefore inscribed in the text in an underhand, secretive manner, thus linking the two antithetical senses in one single chain that permits the exchange of incompatible qualities: if repose can be hot and active without however losing its distinctive virtue of tranquility, then the 'real' activity can lose its fragmentary and dispersed quality and become whole without having to be any less real.[12]

De Man's analysis is intended to effect a demystification of the authority of metaphor as a paradigm of poetic language. If the movement of metaphor in Proust (one of arbitrary substitutions and displacements) is not idiosyncratic, as de Man believes it is not, then there is no real difference between metaphor and metonymy. Metaphor is nothing more than dissembled metonymy. The distinction between metaphor and metonymy in de Man's argument corresponds to his distinction between symbol and allegory. Whereas the symbol deceptively implies the unity between signifier and signified, allegory dualistically and ironically implies the division between them.

Metaphor is not alone affected by this understanding. Self, will, narrative: the tropes that make coherent and bestow value on our experience, according to the common (i.e., naive) understanding can be demystified. In a discussion of Nietzsche's *The Birth of Tragedy*, de Man deconstructs an assertion which becomes for him a statement about the process of deconstruction itself. "This process is an artistic game that the will, in the eternal plenitude of its pleasure, plays with itself." De Man characterizes the "formulation as one in which every word is ambivalent and enigmatic,

[12] Ibid., pp. 65-66.

since the will has been discredited as a self, the pleasure shown to be a lie, the fullness to be absence of meaning, and the play the endless tension of a non-identity, a pattern of dissonance that contaminates the very source of the will, the will as source."[13]

The deconstruction, however, should not end here, for one can perceive de Man's own discourse deconstructing itself. After remarking of the formulation that it is ambivalent and enigmatic, he speaks of it unambivalently and perspicuously: the will is discredited, pleasure a lie, plenitude an absence. This does not count as a polemical point against de Man, because intrinsic to the deconstructive enterprise is a sophisticated awareness of the problematic character of all discourse, including its own. If all discourse is in practice at odds with its own "intention," why shouldn't deconstructive discourse suffer the same fate? In fact, every problematic of discourse becomes, as it were, evidence for the deconstructive view. Thus de Man is legitimately without surprise when a deconstructive critic of his text remarks an unmastered equivocation in his use of the word "error."[14]

The effect of a deconstructive analysis is to convert or reduce the thematic variety of texts to the deconstructive process. Nature in Rousseau, for example, is not so much a theme as a function that deconstructs an artificial system, fragmenting its illusory wholeness. Deconstructive success may lead to a complacency in which "the natural state" becomes another artificial system, which in turn invites deconstruction. "Deconstruction engenders endless other 'natures' in an eternally repeated pattern of regression."[15] Nature then becomes a metaphor for the deconstructive process itself.

Deconstruction abhors identity and consonance. It drives

[13] Ibid., p. 99.

[14] See Stanley Corngold, "Error in Paul de Man" and "A Letter from Paul de Man," *Critical Inquiry* 8 (Spring 1982), 489-513.

[15] De Man, *Allegories of Reading*, p. 249.

a wedge into unity, wherever it finds it, fragmenting the unity into difference, or, rather, it releases elements in what is intrinsically an unstable unity. The task of deconstruction is endless, because the emptiness that would resolve all contradictions is unreachable within the space of language. Language, as Saussure taught, is a system of differences, each term in the system itself an unstable element and therefore no element at all, since it can again be divided. Deconstruction so conceived is an inversion of the Hegelian dialectic. "If there were a definition of difference," Derrida writes, "it would be precisely the limit, the interruption, the destruction of the Hegelian *relève* [*Aufhebung*] wherever it operates."[16] Each term in the Hegelian dialectic is conceived as an unstable unity of opposites or differences, which can be progressively reconciled or synthesized on higher and higher levels. Unlike the Hegelian dialectic, which achieves its resolutions in totality, deconstruction is an endlessly regressive process with nothingness as its unreachable goal.

The movement of deconstruction is a stripping away, an unceasing reduction to elements and of elements, an admittedly vain attempt to dissolve the elements. Deconstruction may carry within it the metaphysical desire to achieve an erasure of error and falsity, but no matter how rigorous its exercise, it is in de Man's words "powerless to prevent the unwarranted identifications achieved by substitution even in its own discourse and to uncross, so to speak, the aberrant exchanges that have taken place."[17] The best deconstruction can do is to acknowledge and specify as precisely as it can the duplicitous condition of discourse.

What deconstruction uncovers is a virtually automatic process in discourse in which subject and intention, factors external to the linguistic function, become irrelevant. Not

[16] Jacques Derrida, *Positions*, trans. Alan Bass (Chicago: University of Chicago Press, 1981), pp. 40-41. Could it be that Derrida illicitly conflates difference and contradiction? Difference is possible without contradiction.

[17] *Allegories of Reading*, p. 242.

that de Man denies the possibility of nonlinguistic motives. Thus he speaks of Marcel's guilt "about his flight away from 'the real' activity of the outward world" and goes on to characterize "the passage on reading" as an attempt to reconcile "imagination and action and to resolve the ethical conflict that exists between them."[18] De Man notes that, in *A la recherche du temps perdu*, "guilt is always centered on reading and on writing, which the novel so often evokes in somber tones. This connection between metaphor and guilt is one of the recurrent themes of autobiographical fiction." But at the same time he is careful to resist the view that the rhetorical strategy is caused by a nonlinguistic motive.

> One should not conclude that the subjective feelings of guilt motivate the rhetorical strategies as causes determine effects . . . no one can decide whether Proust invented metaphors because he felt guilty or whether he had to declare himself guilty in order to find a use for his metaphors. Since the only irreducible "intention" of a text is that of its constitution, the second hypothesis is in fact less unlikely than the first.

De Man avoids out-and-out linguistic determinism by leaving the problem "suspended in its own indecision," but it is clear that he is strongly inclined to the second hypothesis. In fact, rhetoric is a function of indecision. It arises "when it is impossible to decide by grammatical or other linguistic devices which of two meanings (that can be entirely incompatible) prevails. Rhetoric radically suspends logic and opens up vertiginous possibilities of referential aberration."[19]

The extraordinary episode in *The Confessions* in which Rousseau falsely accuses a maid of stealing a ribbon that he himself stole, becomes for de Man a model for the text as a self-generating machine. "The structure is self-perpetuating, *en abîme*, as is implied in its description as ex-

[18] Ibid., pp. 64-65.
[19] Ibid., p. 10.

posure of the desire to expose, for each new stage in the unveiling suggests a deeper shame, a greater impossibility to reveal, and a greater satisfaction in outwitting this impossibility."[20] Rousseau's confession of his guilt and the "self"-revelation that occurs in consequence is neither intentional nor referential. It is the text that endlessly generates its themes and arguments through the mechanical interplay of grammatical entities.

Reader-oriented criticism (in Fish's version) makes the author disappear. Deconstructive criticism in a sense makes the reader disappear. The deconstructive "reader" extinguishes his own values and interests (or at least attempts to do so) and enters into complicity with the deconstructive process of the text itself. The great texts (the deconstructive canon) are those that know their own incoherence, in which case the critic is only a catalyst of the text's own deconstructions. Thus Hillis Miller celebrates "great works of literature as being ahead of their critics."

> They are there already. They have anticipated explicitly any deconstruction the critic can achieve. A critic may hope with great effort, and with the indispensable help of the writers themselves, to raise himself to the level of linguistic sophistication where Chaucer, Spenser, Shakespeare, Milton, Wordsworth, George Eliot, Stevens, or even Williams are already. They are there already.[21]

The disappearance of the reader is symmetrical with the disappearance of the author. If the text is without an author, "reading" necessarily should be without a reader. (In

[20] Ibid., p. 286.

[21] J. Hillis Miller, "Deconstructing the Deconstructors," review of Joseph N. Riddel's *The Inverted Bell*, in *Diacritics* 5 (Summer 1975), 31. Riddel argues that deconstruction is betrayed when "it preserves and recanonizes the great writers and tradition." "A Miller's Tale," *Diacritics* 5 (Fall 1975), 63. But given the logic of deconstruction, which occurs inside the linguistic activity of the text, it is hard to imagine an alternative to preservation, or at least to preservation under erasure.

speaking of "the critic" and "the writers themselves" Miller seems to forget the autonomous life that texts are presumed to have.) Deconstruction smokes out the subject from its last refuge—the reader. All that remains is the text unravelling itself. Deconstruction is a process without authorial or readerly *authority*. The determinism of the linguistic function displaces the determinations of authors and readers.

In treating the texts of "Descrates," "Leibniz," "Rousseau," or "Hegel," Derrida frees them from authorial determination by evaporating the very idea of author. If, as Michel Foucault remarks, "the author allows a limitation of the cancerous and dangerous proliferation of significations within a world where one is thrifty not only with one's resources and riches, but also with one's discourse and their significations,"[22] the effect of evaporating the author, it would seem, is to free discourse to enact the proliferation of "meaning" interminably. But the proliferation cannot escape what Derrida calls "the metaphysical closure" constituted by the series of texts. "*All concepts hitherto proposed in order to think the articulation of a discourse and of an historical totality are caught within the metaphysical closure that I question here*. . . . we do not know of any other concepts and cannot produce any others, and indeed shall not produce so long as this closure limits our discourse."[23]

The deconstructive task, of course, is to disrupt the closure, but since each gap or opening closes in a new way, the deconstructionist remains, so to speak, parasitically attached to every new version of the closure, endlessly performing the disruptive function. Even the novelty of his vocabulary (difference, trace, supplement) are the names for functions already implicit in the structures he is addressing, for what distinguishes a "canonical" text is that it

[22] Michel Foucault, "What Is an Author," in *Textual Strategies*, ed. Josue V. Harari (Ithaca, N.Y.: Cornell University Press, 1979), pp. 144-45.

[23] Jacques Derrida, *Of Grammatology*, trans. Gayatri Spivak (Baltimore: The Johns Hopkins University Press, 1976), p. 99.

knowingly deconstructs itself.[24] The texts of Derrida remain "caught within the metaphysical closure" that they question. Any effort to get beyond it would involve a gesture of transcendence for which there is no provision in the deconstructive method.

Thus de Man takes a text with established authority, like Proust's *Remembrance of Things Past* or Rousseau's *Social Contract,* in which a theme or question is reflectively treated in an imaginative or philosophic context without any questioning, rigorous or otherwise, of the value of the text or of any text for his explorations. In establishing a true or exemplary reading of the text, assuming that he succeeds in doing so, de Man feels entitled to leap to a philosophical conclusion about the theme or question treated. What Proust has to say about metaphor, or rather what de Man is able to discover about metaphor through deconstructing the presentation of metaphoric activity in a passage from *Remembrance of Things Past,* becomes a paradigm for the understanding of metaphor—as a dissembling of metonymy. What is not established, however, is the exemplary character of this particular "metaphoric" activity.

Similarly, nature is seen as receiving its fragmentary meaning from a deconstruction of its particular role in *The Social Contract.* The implicit assumption is that the deconstructive process as it operates within or on a text elicits essential thought or thinking about the theme. If nature is not an empirical object but a category of thought (to be understood, for instance, in a binary opposition to art or culture or the supernatural), then the authority of a text is in its capacity to constitute the category. De Man writes as if Rousseau invented nature. This allows him to make an exemplary reading of Rousseau's text coextensive with the interrogation of nature. The "scholastic" habit of the

[24] Thus in *Blindness and Insight* (New York: Oxford University Press, 1971), de Man criticizes Derrida for not perceiving that Derrida's deconstruction of a text by Rousseau has already been anticipated by Rousseau.

deconstructionist is not fortuitous: it results from an evaporation of the subject in both its authorial and its readerly form. All that is left is the text.

The "ultimate" quarry of the deconstructionist is truth itself, and for this pursuit he has no less of an authority than Nietzsche, who calls into question the very axiom that constitutes the possibility of truth: "the principle of noncontradiction." The following quotations are from a posthumous passage by Nietzsche, which de Man cites, that are part of the case against truth or rather the will-to-truth.

> . . . The question remains open: are the axioms of logic adequate to reality or are they a means and measure for us to *create* the real, the concept of "reality" for ourselves? . . . to affirm the former one would, as already stated, we have to have a previous knowledge of entities; which is certainly not the case. The proposition therefore contains no *criterion of truth*, but an imperative concerning that which should count as true. . . .
>
> The very first acts of thought, affirmation, and denial, holding true and not holding true, are, inasmuch as they presuppose [*voraussetzen*] not only the habit of holding them not true, but the *right* to do so, already dominated by the belief that *there is such a thing as knowledge for us and that judgments really can reach the truth*:—in short, logic does not doubt its ability to assert something about the true-in-itself (namely that it *can* not have opposite attributes).
>
> Here *reigns* the coarse sensualistic preconception that sensations teach us *truths* about things—that I cannot say at the same time of one and the same thing that it is *hard* and that it is *soft*. (The instinctive proof "I cannot have two opposite sensations at the same time"—*quite coarse* and *false*.)
>
> The conceptual ban on contradictions proceeds from the belief that we can *form* concepts, that the concept not only designates [*bezeichnen*] the essence of a thing but

comprehends it [*fassen*] . . . In fact, logic (like geometry and arithmetic) applies only to *fictitious truths [fingierte Wahrheiten] that we have created.* Logic is the attempt to *understand the actual world by means of a scheme of being posited [gesetzt] by ourselves, more correctly to make it easier to formalize and compute [berechnen] . . .*[25]

De Man points out that Nietzsche elsewhere extends his attack upon the authority of conceptualization, i.e., knowledge, to "the epistemological authority of perception and of eudaemonic patterns of experience."[26] According to de Man, no one before Nietzsche (and perhaps no one after him) has so forcefully driven a wedge between consciousness and reality. Yet if "thinking . . . is a quite arbitrary function, arrived at by singling out one element from the process and eliminating all the rest, an artificial arrangement for the purpose of intelligibility," what is the status of the deconstructive thinking that has produced this thought? The deconstructive act is the consciousness of the deceit, the awareness of all the contingencies and accidents that are concealed and falsified for the sake of intelligibility. In the interest of what? One could hardly say truth, since truth has become deceit. Indeed, it is a question whether one can speak of deceit since the term itself implies the existence of truth. In the interests of what, then? It is the process itself that is valued, the rigor and perseverance with which the deconstructionist pursues his activity. Nietzsche himself was at times willing to come to rest in value terms—like strength, health, distinction. But the deconstructionist scorns both the values and the repose implied by the values. "Nietzsche's critique is not conducted in the tone and by means of the arguments usually associated with classical critical philosophy. It is often carried on by means of such pragmatic and demagogical value oppositions as weakness and strength, disease and health, herd and the happy few,

[25] De Man, *Allegories of Reading*, pp. 120-21.
[26] Ibid., p. 123.

terms so arbitrarily valorized that it becomes difficult to take them seriously."[27]

Despite the cognitive "passion" of deconstruction, it is singularly barren in producing cognitive results. The information that a text provides is either uninteresting or suspect, since what counts is the deceptive play of language. In severing the text from the reality to which it might refer, the text does not offer any knowledge of our experience of the world—except the negative knowledge of unreliability and deceptiveness. In other words, the cognitive interest of deconstruction leads to the knowledge that we can have no real knowledge. In saying that deconstruction is barren of cognitive results I don't mean to suggest that deconstructive readings of individual works cannot be illuminating. But what they illuminate is difference, incoherence, and so forth, features shared by all works and which, paradoxically, erase the differences between works. What is accomplished by textual analysis in the deconstructive mode is not an understanding of the particular text but a theoretical reflection on the deliberately erroneous claims that the text makes about itself. To the extent that deconstruction is faithful to (or accurate in describing) difference et cetera, it does produce cognitive results, but I would insist that such knowledge is barren because it is monotonously repetitious in its results.

For all its suspicion of truth claims, deconstructionist thought usually has a resemblance to the truth it has deconstructed: it, too, is capable of intelligibility, despite the stylistic exertions of deconstructionists. If one considers the terms that have been put into question: intelligibility, plenitude, self, will, purposiveness (teleology), it is surprising how formidable they are in the texts that purport to deconstruct them. It is as if the deconstructive will has encountered in the will-to-"truth" (granting for a moment the epistemological premises of deconstructionist thought) an

[27] Ibid., p. 119.

immovable object. That is to say, the will-to-truth is simply the will-to-make-sense, to create order out of the chaos of things: it is the will-to-order, whether the order is "true" or "false." How fastidious, orderly (and teleological?) the deconstructionist is in dismantling the text and how discriminating in his judgments of terms and arguments. Rigor, subtlety (sometimes devalorized by the term deviousness or duplicity), intelligence, sophistication (the opposite of naiveté) remain undeconstructed value terms in deconstructionist discourse. Given the necessity of discourse, how could they fail to be?

Here I think we reach the limit of the deconstructive capacity to anticipate and disarm all criticism. This capacity does not extend to the values that govern the deconstructive process, values that of necessity remain undeconstructed. That is, since the values are more than linguistic functions and deconstruction occurs exclusively within the space of language, no deconstruction can either make or unmake the values that determine its own discourse. Rigor and sophistication, for example, are expressions of will and are the cause of other rhetorical functions in the discourse they occupy. In saying this, one is introducing the disreputable, if not discredited, transcendental value-making agency in the discussion—unavoidably it seems to me.

As I noted earlier, de Man argues that the question of what determines rhetorical strategy is undecidable, but then goes on to decide that language determines its own strategy. It would seem, however, that the necessity and presence of values in discourse would require a subjective cause for rhetorical strategy. If health, strength, and distinction (Nietzsche's value terms) have been "arbitrarily valorized" (as de Man claims) doesn't the judgment imply not simply value, but value that is not arbitrarily valorized, that is persuasive, necessary—whatever opposes arbitrariness? The tropological machine that makes for substitutions and displacements can hardly be expected to generate the terms that are the very foundation of the activity that uncovers them; unless, of course, rigor and sophistication merely produce an endless play of tropes in which the only advantage a trope or fragment has over another trope or fragment is that it has provisionally succeeded it. Rigor and sophistication in that case would be as illusory as any other tropes.

Deconstruction is an activity of questioning and subversion. It neither constitutes nor authorizes anything.

> What is questioned by the thought of differance . . . is the determination of being in presence . . . the first consequence of this is that differance is not. It is not a being-present. . . . It commands nothing, rules over nothing, and nowhere does it exercise any authority. It is not marked by a capital letter. Not only is there no realm of differance, but differance is even the subversion of every realm. This is *obviously* [my emphasis] what makes it threatening and necessarily dreaded by everything in us that desires a realm . . .[28]

I have italicized *obviously* because it is a word of authoritative certainty of which Derrida declares himself to be a particularly vigilant critic. "For my part, wherever and whenever I hear the words 'it's true,' 'it's false,' 'it's evident,' 'evidently this or that,' or 'in a fairly obvious way' I become suspicious."[29] Derrida, of course, does not deny his own susceptibility to the language of certainty, authority, and centrality. He even admits in characteristically disarming fashion the pragmatic necessity of all the terms that he deconstructs.

> I didn't say that there was no center. I believe that the center is not a being—a reality, but a function. But this

[28] Jacques Derrida, "Differance" in *Speech and Phenomena and other essays on Husserl's Theory of Signs*, trans. David B. Allison (Evanston, Ill.: Northwestern University Press, 1973), p. 133.

[29] "Limited Inc. abc," in *Glyph 2* (Baltimore: The Johns Hopkins University Press, 1977), p. 175.

> function is absolutely indispensable. The subject is absolutely indispensable. I don't destroy it; I situate it.[30]

Derrida implies that the contingencies and conventions of cultural life do not preclude the possibility of truth, rightness, naturalness (authoritative terms) within that life.

But the admission does not or should not disarm criticism. What does it mean to situate "the function of authority"? Where is its situation? If "differance is . . . the subversion of every realm," how does authority ("the center") continue to exercise its indispensable function? Derrida's pragmatic awareness consists in what we all intuit to be the poverty and unhappiness of "the thought of difference." For what does it mean to command nothing and deny authority? It means to claim powerlessness, which is no happy condition, even if others take no advantage of our condition; if others do take advantage, it is a miserable condition. Authority, as Derrida knows, is connected with all the value terms that make life tolerable: meaning, truth, purpose. How can the thought of difference fail to undermine the function of authority, if the function is based on nothing?

Derrida writes, as he must write, in an authoritative way—in unequivocal positives and negatives—as if he were speaking from a ground that transcends difference. Frank Lentricchia's criticism of other deconstructionist critics who ignore or avoid Derrida's anti-authoritative argument and "have taken difference as a radically subversive authority which autocratically commands as *abyme*, the whole field of writing"[31] misses the paradoxical condition of "the thought of difference," which Derrida shares with all deconstructionists. I have tried to show that even in the thoroughgoing skepticism of deconstruction the values and interests that

[30] *The Structuralist Controversy*, ed. Eugenio Donato and Richard Macksey (Baltimore: The Johns Hopkins University Press, 1972), p. 271.

[31] Frank Lentricchia, *After the New Criticism* (Chicago: University of Chicago Press, 1980), p. 173.

determine it (e.g., rigor, sophistication) of necessity have their source in an undeconstructible authoritative space beyond skeptical activity itself.

In a rare passage in *Allegories of Reading*, de Man makes a claim for the constitutive, value-making side of deconstruction.

> Within the epistemological labyrinth of figural structures, recuperation of selfhood would be accomplished by the rigor with which the discourse deconstructs the very notion of the self. The originator of this discourse is then no longer the dupe of his own wishes; he is as far beyond pleasure and pain as he is beyond good and evil or, for that matter, beyond strength and weakness. His consciousness is neither happy nor unhappy, nor does he possess any power. He remains however a center of authority to the extent that the very destructiveness of his ascetic reading testifies to the validity of his interpretation. The dialectical reversal that transfers the authority from experience into interpretation and transforms, by a hermeneutic process, the total insignificance, the nothingness of the self into a new center of meaning, is a very familiar gesture in contemporary thought, the ground of what is abusively called modernity.[32]

De Man then proceeds to invoke Paul Ricoeur's conception of Freud in order to establish "the familiarity of the gesture." Freud's analysis of the self "assumes the forgetting and the vacillation of self" (in Ricoeur's phrase). Yet "Freudian deconstruction" (how easily writers are assimilated to the new vocabulary) is the basis for the "recovery of meaning in interpretation and the subject is reborn in the guise of the interpreter."

The process that de Man describes resembles the Cartesian *cogito* in which the self is constituted (or inaugurated) by the very doubt of its existence. In Descartes the verb

[32] De Man, *Allegories of Reading*, pp. 173-74.

"doubt" necessarily assumes the subject "I." The self is thus a logical or grammatical construction of the verb. Unlike the Cartesian ego, however, the deconstructive ego has no existence apart from and independent of its function. The deconstructive self is coterminus in time and space with its activity. What are the attributes or characteristics of the deconstructive "self" beyond its grammatical function? Mobility, elusiveness, a constant though equable suspicion of the illusoriness of everything, so that one is always tempted, if not compelled, to enclose words, including self, in quotation marks. De Man speaks of the "inventive power of the self" as consisting in "the wealth of self-discoveries possible in self-reading," though he also speaks of the impossibility of reading. Elusive and evanescent, self and meaning have no more substantiality than the words themselves. All the anxieties that might be increased by a deconstructive rigor disappear, because, one surmises, they are based on assumptions about the self that deconstruction has undone. The spiritual character of deconstructive equanimity is fittingly described as ascetic, but not ascetic (as one finds in the onto-theological dispensation) in behalf of a greater plenitude that will fill the vessel once it has been emptied. The movement is toward nothingness, which lies on the other side of language, if not in language itself.

De Man's model of the self is based entirely on the logic of the linguistic function of deconstruction. Since all subjective, transcendent considerations are ruled out of court, we are not able to address in a fruitful way questions that would arise in any familiar (naive) discourse about what it means to have a self, to be alive, to hope, to have ambition and so on. Is it possible or desirable to possess a consciousness that is neither happy nor unhappy, that is content (even this word is insufficiently neutral) with powerlessness? And if it were possible for the extraordinary few (extraordinary in that they are out of the ordinary), why should this model be a value? The weakness or limitation of deconstruction, as I have said, is that it is powerless to address in its own terms questions about its own values.

The theoretical dissolution of the self in deconstructive theory does not eliminate the self in deconstructive practice. Attitude, tone of voice, the particular character of language conspire to compose a self, which we can hear and respond to. The undeconstructible self that writes circumscribes the deconstructive assault on the text. Deconstruction wants to say, in defiance of the idiom of natural language, that "writing selves" (selves here understood as a verb), whereas natural language teaches that the self writes.

There are temperamental differences between deconstructionists, but if an idea can be said to have a temperament, de Man, I think, best exemplifies the temperament of deconstruction, despite the fact that its seminal figure is Derrida. Though he affirms the "privileged status of literature" and speaks of literature as "an authentic language," the effect of de Man's performance is an attack upon literature. All the qualities of imagination, feeling, and intellect that have been the source of the power and appeal of literature are seen as illusory. As de Man would have it, we must resist the blandishments of literature in the interest of philosophical rigor. More consistent than Plato, who betrayed a love for poetry despite his philosophical hatred of it by the eloquence of his own dramatic imagination, de Man in a deliberately arid style shows in the machinelike march of arguments his anti-literary colors very clearly. The deconstructive critic is a philosopher *manqué*, committed as he is to truth or logic, which he nevertheless declares to be impossible because of the tropological nature of all discourse.

In an essay "The Resistance to Theory," de Man identifies the very idea of literary theory with linguistically-oriented skeptical theory.

> Literary theory can be said to come into being when the approach to literary texts is no longer based on nonlin-

> guistic, that is to say, historical and aesthetic, considerations or, to put it somewhat less crudely, when the object of discussion is no longer the meaning or the value but the modalities of production and of reception of meaning and value prior to their establishment—the implication being that this establishment is problematic enough to require an autonomous discipline of critical investigation to consider its possibility and its status.[33]

Any critique of current literary theory involves a critique of the idea of theory as a demystifying activity. Those who wish to discuss meaning and value, history and aesthetics must now define a theoretical or at least a speculative space of their own, or accept exclusion from the circle of true critical awareness.

In the preceding and ensuing discussions of deconstruction, I have not tried to add to the body of exposition for its own sake. We already have a number of such expositions.[34] My purpose has been to place the deconstructive view in a context of contemporary skepticism in literary study. I have not situated the work of Derrida in the philosophical tradition where it originated and where it ultimately may belong, to use a teleological language that is anathema to deconstruction. If one wishes to learn about Derrida's relation to the French philosophic tradition, one would do well to turn to Vincent Descombes's *Modern French Philosophy*.[35]

It may be that deconstruction as an attitude toward texts constitutes a misappropriation of philosophical concerns to literary practice. The difficulty with this objection is that it rests on an all-too-secure distinction between philosophy and literature which deconstruction seeks to undermine.

[33] Paul de Man, "The Resistance to Theory," *Yale French Studies* 63 (1982), 7.

[34] See in particular Jonathan Culler, *On Deconstruction* (Ithaca, N.Y.: Cornell University Press, 1983) and Christopher Norris, *Deconstruction: Theory and Practice* (London and New York: Methuen, 1982).

[35] (Cambridge: Cambridge University Press, 1982.)

If philosophy is just another kind of writing (Richard Rorty's neat formulation of the deconstructive view), and the subject is writing, then both philosophy and literature are the appropriate concerns of deconstructive criticism.

In writing of deconstruction, one necessarily refers to the work of a number of writers whose differences from one another may be falsified by subsuming them under a unifying term. This is especially the case with an intellectual activity (I hesitate to call it a philosophy) that prides itself on its scrupulous sensitivity to difference. But as even the most thoroughgoing deconstructionists know, these unifying terms are necessary for discourse—that is, necessary for the coherence and intelligibility that make discourse possible. I have tried to attach individual writers, principally Derrida and de Man, to the particular exposition I am making without cancelling the differences between them. In each case, the exposition is determined by my own antithetical view of criticism as an evaluative and interpretive activity.

If de Man receives more attention than Derrida, it is not to deny Derrida's preeminence as the philosopher of deconstruction: it is simply to acknowledge the particular efficacy of de Man's presence in literary study and the way his voice and temperament bring out the ascetic character of deconstructive skepticism. I have not given the kind of attention to Derrida's or de Man's work that I have given to the work of Barthes, simply because Barthes's work is sui generis. It is a career of views, which cannot be expressed as a philosophy to which other writers can attach themselves. In speaking of Derrida, one can often speak, though not always, of deconstruction without naming him. However one wishes to understand the personae of his work, Barthes is the inescapable subject of any discussion of his work. Ironically, the author of "The Death of the Author" is the steady source, the center if you like, of all the decenterings that constitute the career of his texts. Hence his is the only name mentioned in the chapter titles of this book.

6

A QUESTION OF MEANING

The deconstructive view that language, because of its figural deviousness, never coincides with meaning is not unprecedented. The ambition of science to realize itself in the notations of mathematics reflects a suspicion of the treacherous ambiguities of language dating from the seventeenth century. Exponents of the power of poetry have always made a virtue of the equivocations of its language. Meaning is a portentous term against which the literary sensibility has always had a certain prejudice. It connotes gravity and immobility, conditions inimical to imaginative freedom. Meaning is the refuge of those incapable of following flights of imagination. In its opposition to rationalistic discourse, poetry had resisted "the heresy of paraphrase," the idea that poetic expression can be translated into propositional sense. Translation and communication are functions of meaningful discourse, which risk exposing literature to a kind of emptiness. To the extent that literature is translatable into propositional sense, the element of gratuitous play is reduced. There has been a kind of political support for this view, which associates meaning with philistine efforts to sanction the conventional stabilities that betray our authentic meaningless existence.

What distinguishes the deconstructive view from the familiar romantic view of the figural deviousness, richness, and even inadequacy of language is its suspicion (indeed, conviction) that *nothing* underlies the differential play of tropes. It is not simply that language and meaning do not coincide. Meaning, or at least literal meaning, turns out to be an illusion. Such a view depends not only on skepticism about the reliability of language, but about its substantiality as well.

Derrida characterizes the target of the deconstructive critique as "the authority of meaning," which he equates with "the transcendental signified" and with "telos."[1] And elsewhere he writes of the text as questioning not "intention or intentionality but their telos, which orients and organizes the movement and the possibility of a fulfillment, realization and *actualization* in a plenitude that would be *present* to and identical with itself."[2] In other words, Derrida identifies the absence of meaning with the *necessary* failure of the subject (the source of the transcendental signified) to realize its intention within the text. Unlike speech-act theorists, Derrida asserts the impossibility of the fulfillment of intention.

Even if, for the sake of argument, one were to concede the difference between intention and actualization, the term difference covers a variety of cases. Differences may be small or large. Difference may become contradiction, or may be the sheer failure of intention to actualize any part of itself. Or the different realization of a text (beyond its intention, despite its *telos*) may have a richness, a plenitude, though "it might not be identical with itself." The fact of difference between intention and actualization does not extinguish meaning.

Meaning need not be construed to signify merely propositional sense. It can represent the effective power of the text upon the mind of the reader. The strength of an image or the exaltation of a cadence may have an even more persuasive effect upon a reader than the most coherent argument. And if the work does not make easy sense—or sense at all—it may want through the power (if not the

[1] Jacques Derrida, *Positions*, trans. Alan Bass (Chicago: University of Chicago Press, 1981), pp. 48-49.

[2] Jacques Derrida, "Limited Inc. abc" in *Glyph 2* (Baltimore: The Johns Hopkins University Press, 1977), p. 193.

propositional sense) of words to challenge, assault, or revolutionize the consciousness of the reader. It is to this ambition of literature that Lionel Trilling responds when he characterizes modern literature in the following fashion:

> Modern literature (it need scarcely be said again) is directed toward moral and spiritual renovation; its doctrine is damnation and salvation. It is a literature of doctrine, which although often concealed is very aggressive. The occasions are few when criticism has met this doctrine on its own fierce terms. Of modern criticism it can be said that it has instructed us in an intelligent passivity before the beneficent aggression of literature. Attributing to literature virtually angelic powers, it has passed the word to readers of literature that one thing you do not do when you meet an angel is wrestle with him.[3]

The "doctrine" Trilling speaks of need not be explicit in the work: it can be assumed by it (e.g., *The Stranger*) or it can be an element in its dialectic (e.g., *Notes from the Underground*), which is itself the source of the aggressive power of the work. The aggressiveness of the work derives not from its doctrine (its propositional sense), but from the experiential element in the work.

As Jonathan Culler notes, "for the rhetoricians of antiquity and the Renaissance, and for many critics of other times a poem is a composition designed to produce an effect on readers, to move them in certain ways; and one's judgment of a poem depends on one's sense of the quality and intensity of its effect."[4] He then distinguishes this view from the concerns of "modern reader-oriented critics," which he

[3] "The Teaching of Modern Literature," in *Beyond Culture* (New York: Viking Press, 1965), p. 231. This statement, of course, is not without irony. The renovation modern literature affirms is an inversion of traditional Christian ideas.

[4] Jonathan Culler, *On Deconstruction: Theory and Practice after Structuralism* (Ithaca, N.Y.: Cornell University Press, 1982), p. 39.

characterizes as "cognitive rather than affective." The "affective" critic finds in the complex richness of a work the occasion for gratitude, even celebration. The cognitive critic, as Culler represents the case, cannot accept ambiguity, or, worse, ungovernable complexity.

> Acts of interpretation do not necessarily seem to bring us closer to a goal such as a more accurate understanding of all the major works of European literature. Indeed, the cynic might say that criticism does not move forward to better interpretations and fuller understanding so much as toward what Schoenberg achieved in his *Ewartung*: a chromatic plenitude, a playing of all possible registers, a saturation of musical space.[5]

Culler's distinction between the cognitive and the affective is a symptom of the modern view in its dissociation of sensibility. The distinction ignores the possibility of the fusion of feeling and knowing, what Eliot called "felt thought" in his characterization of the metaphysical poets.

In reading *Notes from Underground*, for example one can hardly avoid responding in a way that is at once cognitive and affective. Dostoevsky's underground man concludes with a statement about the "meaning" of his tale, which may be taken as, in a sense, a deconstruction of his doctrine. He has gone further, he tells us, than anyone else in following out the consequences of (utilitarian) ideas which a great number of people of his society share. Though the result of his deconstructive rigor has been a demonstration of his own nullity, he can claim for himself a vitality that the majority of compromised souls lack.

> For my part, I have merely carried to extremes in my life what you have not dared to carry even half-way, and, in addition, you have mistaken your cowardice for com-

[5] Jonathan Culler, *The Pursuit of Signs* (Ithaca, N.Y.: Cornell University Press, 1983), p. 47.

> mon sense and have found comfort in that, deceiving yourselves. So that, as a matter of fact, I seem to be much more alive than you.

The doctrine of suffering which the underground man asserts in the first part of the tale is a deconstruction of the pleasure/pain calculus, which inverts utilitarian values. The underground man reveals the determinism of the pleasure/pain calculus in the coerciveness of the definition of man as a pleasure-seeking animal. The utilitarian pleasure/pain calculus is an example of "the laws of nature," which create an identity between freedom and necessity. The underground man deconstructs this identity by driving a wedge between them. He proposes the counterexample (himself) of a man who deliberately seeks pain to establish both his freedom and individual reality against the generalizing and neutralizing effect of the laws of nature. Yet it becomes clear that this deconstructive act is itself a determined response to the pleasure/pain calculus. The underground man's suffering is no less compulsive than the pleasure-seeking of utilitarianism. The abrupt and arbitrary conclusion of the tale suggests the possibility of further deconstruction, which would be perversely endless, the logical correlative of the virtuosic masochism of the underground man.

The example of *Notes from Underground* is of particular interest, because it exemplifies the ambiguous relation of deconstruction to the theme of freedom. In deconstructing utilitarianism with its totalizing identification of freedom and necessity, the underground man is apparently acting in the interests of freedom. But since his activity is an exercise in negation, it too is caught within the logic of the determinism against which it is reacting. Only if the underground man could *transcend* the circumscribed logic of deconstruction could he hope to achieve genuine freedom. Deconstruction, which at first looks like freedom, turns out to be a determinism from which there is no escape.

What is ultimately at stake is the condition and the goal of freedom: the sense of individual reality which the underground man lacks and to which he aspires. By framing the story as Dostoevsky does with a narrative voice (which is not that of the underground man), Dostoevsky does not allow the deconstructive logic of the underground man to prevail. The tale can be read as a cautionary tale about the risks of deconstruction. And, indeed, as the confession at the end indicates, the underground man would want to break the spell of the logic that undoes him.

The novel itself paradoxically achieves a sense of overwhelming presence. We not only follow the logic of the underground man's thought; we experience it as his emotional and spiritual condition. The final address to the reader implicates him in the dilemmas of the underground man.

In *Saving The Text* (1981), a sympathetic counterstatement to the work of Derrida, Geoffrey Hartman speaks of the wounding power of the word. His instances come from the great works of literature, the plays of Aeschylus and Shakespeare, the poems of Blake, the novels of Tolstoy and Faulkner. The wounding words are curses, obscenities, piercing insights expressed in language; there are also healing words: blessings, praisings. Hartman means to show, against representational theory, that words are not as neutral and as objective as they appear. But he also shows in the process that they are full of meaning and power. Hartman is stating literature's understanding of its own power. If one assumes that a work or text is full, or at least not empty, then it possesses expressive force, whether or not that force can be translated into propositional sense. Literature may console or provoke or assault. All these powers of literature imply the experience of its plenitude.

The work of Lawrence provides a vividly explicit instance of this understanding. In *Women in Love*, Ursula listens to one of Birkin's characteristic speeches about the death process "only half attentive, half avoiding what he said . . . She listened, making out what he said. She knew as well as he knew, that words themselves do not convey meaning, that they are but a gesture we make, a dumb show like any other. And she seemed to feel his gesture through her blood, and she drew back, even though her desire sent her forward." Ursula challenges Birkin in his inconsistency, reminding him of something apparently contradictory that he had said earlier. Birkin "turned in confusion," silently acknowledging "the confusion of speech. Yet it must be spoken. Whichever way one moved, if one were to move forwards, one must break a way through. And to know, to give utterance, was a way through the walls of the prison as the infant in labour strives through the walls of the womb. There is no new movement now, without the breaking through of the old body, deliberately, in knowledge, in the struggle to get out." Toward the end of the novel, Gudrun effectively challenges Ursula's utopian ambition to enter "a new space."

> "One wants a new space to be in, I quite agree," she said. "But I think that a new world is a development from this world, and that to isolate onself with one other person, isn't to find a new world at all, but only to secure oneself in one's illusions."

The coherence of this statement is unlike the confusion in Birkin's earlier statements, but Ursula again experiences the force of the words in nonpropositional or nonconceptual terms—though her response is quite different from the earlier one. "Ursula looked out of the window. In her soul she began to wrestle, and she was frightened. She was always frightened of words, because she knew that mere word-force could always make her believe what she did not believe." Here silent conviction for the moment resists word-force. Lawrence (or Ursula) is in the romantic tradition, acknowledging the inadequacies as well as the eventfulness of words. The inadequacies, however, are not to be confused with the defectiveness and ultimate nullity that inheres in language according to the deconstructive view.

In acknowledging the truth of deconstructive critique, Harold Bloom defines its limitation. "For the deconstructive critique a trope is a figure of knowing and not a figure of will, and so such a critic seeks to achieve, in relation to any poem—or to find in that poem—a cognitive moment, a moment in which the Negative is realized, but only insofar as a postponing substitution becomes an approximation of the Hegelian Negative."[6] For the pragmatic Bloom, the trope is a figure of will, not of knowing, and he challenges deconstruction with rhetorical questions:

> But what can a cognitive or epistemological moment in a poem be? Where the will predominates, even in its own despite, how much is there left to know? How can we speak of degrees of knowing in the blind world of the wish, where the truth is always elsewhere, always different, always to be encountered only by the acceptances and rejections of an energy that in itself is the anti-thesis of renunciation, a force that refuses all form?

Bloom shares the deconstructive view that the text is a dead letter, an emptiness. And as I have already suggested, his work can be seen in a theological or anti-theological perspective. But he swerves (a Bloomian trope) from the problem of skepticism through a curious ambiguity in his conception of the poetic past. The past as incarnated by great poets is at once an emptiness and a power. It is cognitively and perhaps affectively empty, but remains nevertheless a formidable force of will that has to be overcome and denied by the latecomer. Bloom expresses the ambiguity in terms that are at once Oedipal and theological: "Satan is the modern poet, while God is his dead but still

[6] Harold Bloom, *Wallace Stevens: The Poems of Our Climate* (Ithaca, N.Y.: Cornell University Press, 1977), p. 387.

embarrassingly potent and present ancestor, or rather ancestral poet."[7] Bloom's theoretical "ethic" is one of survival through the assertion of power. Though he denies that poetry is a source of knowledge or faith, he does not declare himself a skeptic in either the epistemological or the theological sense. Bloom's "situation" is characterized by skepticism, but he rejects or tries to reject it through whatever strength and cunning the imagination provides. He cultivates illusions without illusion. "Where the precursor was, there the ephebe shall be, but by the discontinuous mode of emptying the precursor of *his* divinity, while appearing to empty himself of his own."[8] His last resort is the imaginative will.

Of course, Bloom's pragmatic distinction between willing and knowing can be countered by the Nietzschean perception of the will that underlies all human activities, including the will-to-know. To collapse the distinction between knowing and willing is to deny to deconstruction its epistemological privilege; it is also to restore (against its self-understanding) the subject to its own discourse even when the discourse is most impeccably deconstructive. Finally, it is to allow the question, what does deconstruction mean, for meaning depends upon the willing subject. In *Saving the Text*, Hartman characterizes Derrida's prose as entombing "the words of the dead . . . by inner quotation, allusion, or the verbatim presence of a piece of precursor"[9] in a way that Joyce entombs literature in *Finnegans Wake*. In Derrida the appropriation of the philosophical or literary past is not to revive it (make it live in the present), but to eviscerate it—to empty it of whatever seductive power it may have. The "words of the dead" are not beyond reviving, and if Derrida chooses to entomb them, he is engaged in an ac-

[7] Harold Bloom, *The Anxiety of Influence* (New York: Oxford University Press, 1973), p. 20.

[8] Ibid., p. 91.

[9] Geoffrey Hartman, *Saving The Text* (Baltimore: The Johns Hopkins University Press, 1981), p. 80.

tivity against the fullness and vitality of literature. He does not simply discover or reveal the intrinsic emptiness of the text. The deconstructive act is willful, as Derrida acknowledges: "why engage in a work of deconstruction, rather than leave things the way they are? Nothing, here, without a 'show of force' somewhere. Deconstruction, I have insisted, is not *neutral*. It intervenes."[10]

In denying the effective intention of a text (that which originates its substance), deconstruction expresses its own intention: which is to unravel or disintegrate the text. If deconstruction has an intention, it can be said to have a goal, one that it can never reach. It moves backward, rather than forward, to an unreachable origin, "proves" by its endless activity that there is no origin. Though deconstructive activity is interminable (and therefore strictly speaking has no *telos*), its movement to the extent that it is successful is in the direction of its intention. The demonstration of the endlessness of deconstructive activity is the goal of deconstructive teleology.

If deconstruction proposes the most radical attack on meaning (or the meaningfulness of literature), the subversion of meaning in literature is already implicit in the structuralist project. The structuralist rejects the visible meanings of individual works as a diversion from an understanding of the conditions of meaning. Why? The answer is implicit in the structuralist understanding of forms of experience, of which textual activity is an instance. The meaning constituted in the individual text is a sort of mystification of the process by which it is constituted. One already sees the deconstructive tendency in Lévi-Strauss's reconstruction of the Oedipus myth. Lévi-Strauss regards the surface of the myth as a unilinear series of events, which is unintelligible until it has been deconstructed and reassembled into a series of columns.

[10] Derrida, *Positions*, p. 93.

Cadmos seeks his sister, Europa, ravished by Zeus			
		Cadmos kills the dragon	
	The Spartoi kill one another		
			Labdacos (Laios' father) = *lame* (?)
	Oedipus kills his father, Laios		Laios (Oedipus' father) *left-sided* (?)
		Oedipus kills the Sphinx	
			Oedipus = *swollen-foot* (?)
Oedipus marries his mother, Jocasta			
	Eteocles kills his brother, Polyneices		
Antigone buries her brother, Polyneices, despite prohibition			

We thus find ourselves confronted with four vertical columns each of which includes several relations belonging to the same bundle. Were we to *tell* the myth, we would disregard the columns and read the rows from left to right and from top to bottom. But if we want to *understand* the myth, then we will have to disregard one half of the diachronic dimension (top to bottom) and read from left to right, column after column, each one being considered as a unit.[11]

[11] Claude Lévi-Strauss, *Structural Anthropology* (New York: Basic Books, 1963). p. 214.

Against the surface structure proposed by the myth, Lévi-Strauss offers what he considers to be its true structure. His claim to have discovered the true structure, and the rigidity of the structure, make him antithetical to deconstruction, but if one disregards the claim of truth and the rigidity of the structure, one has before the reconstruction a version of the deconstructive "method." Lévi-Strauss himself is sensitive to what may be called deconstructive entropy. This sensitivity qualifies the essentially constitutive tendency of his work.

> There is no real end to mythological analysis, no hidden unity to be grasped once the breaking down process has been completed. . . . The unity of a myth is never more than tendential and cannot reflect a state or a particular moment of the myth. It is a phenomenon of the imagination, resulting from the attempt at interpretation; and its function is to endow the myth with synthetic form and to prevent its disintegration into a confusion of opposites. . . . Since it has no interest in definite beginnings or endings, mythological thought never develops any theme to completion: There is always something left unfinished. Myths, like rites, are "interminable."[12]

In any event, the surface of the text, i.e., the meaning and experience it proposes, is immediately the object of suspicion. The surface, however, is not denied, it is rather broken up, so that it can be reconstructed (for the structuralist) and further deconstructed (for the deconstructionist).

It is possible to argue as Jonathan Culler does that deconstruction takes an interest in the surface of a text in a way in which traditional serious philosophical discourse does not. "Unwilling to renounce the possibilities of serious argument or the claim to deal with essential matters, decon-

[12] See Frank Lentricchia, *After The New Criticism* (Chicago: University of Chicago Press, 1980), p. 126.

struction nevertheless attempts to escape the confines of the serious since it also disputes the priority accorded to 'serious' philosophical considerations over matters of, shall we say, linguistic 'surface.' "[13] One should point out, however, that the attention to surface is a suspicious one. Thus the differences elicited within a metaphor that purports to bind two terms in a unity is a demystification of the surface claim of the metaphor, a penetration to a level below the surface.

The quality or texture of the work disappears in both the structuralist and the deconstructive analysis. In breaking up a whole into parts or unraveling the strands that compose a work, one may suggest the sensuous character of a part or strand and what it might have contributed to the total effect of the work. "Traditional" criticism can give us the pleasure of the element. Like structuralism, deconstruction takes pleasure only in its own activity. In structuralism, the whole is a construction that has lost touch with surface, the texture of the original work. In deconstruction, the trace of the whole, of the deconstructed part, is volatilized to the point where it loses its hold on our imagination.

In *Science and the Modern World* Alfred North Whitehead criticized modern science for having split the object world between primary qualities (density, mass, extension), qualities subject to scientific understanding and secondary qualities (color, texture, smell, sound, etc.), the sensuous "data" of our experience. According to Whitehead, the poetry of Wordsworth and Shelley was a valuable attempt to restore the object to wholeness so that it could be simultaneously experienced and understood.[14] Wordsworth proposed po-

[13] Culler, *On Deconstruction*, p. 151.

[14] See Alfred North Whitehead, *Science and the Modern World* (New York: Macmillan, 1948). The split that Whitehead discerned was described by T. S. Eliot as a "dissociation of sensibility." For Eliot romantic poetry, whatever its programmatic intentions, was a symptom, not a remedy, and his own effort as a poet was to re-create the fusion of intellect and feeling which in his view belonged to metaphysical poetry of the seventeenth century before the dissociation had occurred.

etry as a rival, not as a complementary, activity to science. Whitehead's proposal that Wordsworth's conception of poetry be considered as a possible path that modern science might take has long seemed quixotic and irrelevant. If Whitehead's argument had any effect, it was to remind readers of the impact of romantic poetry, which Arnold has beautifully expressed in his "Memorial Verses" on the death of Wordsworth.

> Our youth returned; for there was shed
> On spirits that had long been dead,
> Spirits dried up and closely furled,
> The freshness of the early world.

It is an irony of literary history that the vanguard of literary study has come to occupy a position similar to that of science in the romantic argument against it. In its unconcern with the experience of literature, structuralism and deconstruction show their affinity with science, dividing texts, so to speak, into their primary and secondary qualities. Secondary qualities are what we naively experience; primary qualities are inaccessible to feeling, but they constitute the "truth" of the text which the secondary qualities mystify. Deconstruction is anti-scientific in its suspicion of the very idea of truth, its animus against structure and method. Yet it is not fortuitous that deconstruction is contemporary with the effort to establish criticism on a scientific basis. Deconstruction may criticize such an effort, but the criticism is weakened by its complicity with scientific *rigor* and its animus against the experience of literature. Both structuralism and deconstruction have anti-phenomenological implications. Deconstruction inherits the structuralist distinction between the *réel* and the *vécu.* In order to arrive at the *réel* (whether it is conceived as a plenitude or an absence), one must reject the *vécu* (experience), the ultimate data of phenomenological inquiry, as illusory. For deconstruction, there is no *réel,* no primary qualities to be discovered. What remains is the paradoxical texture, the illusory substance of deconstructive activity itself.

Despite Hillis Miller's claim that it is criticism itself or criticism fully conscious of and rigorous in its activity, deconstruction hardly exhausts the possibilities of criticism—even when its rigor is impeccable. Its analytical goal is not the breaking down of the parts that make the whole in order to show the elements of which the whole is constituted, a traditional task of criticism. Its goal is rather to show the whole as a meretricious fabrication of parts that are in a sense falsified when brought together. Deconstruction is hostile to the constitutive aspect of the poetic faculty. It shows no inclination to account for the power or vitality of the metaphor, the coherence of self, the teleology of narrative, the meaningfulness of meaning.

It is possible to be an anti-theological skeptic without being a demystifier or deconstructionist. Kenneth Burke, who calls himself a linguistic skeptic, has no illusions about the origins of god terms. Like the deconstructionists, he knows that words are not handed down from heaven, that they are derived from "the realm of our everyday experiences."[15] Supernatural language, once generated, has a verbal and emotive dynamic of its own and becomes susceptible in turn to an appropriation by the everyday realm. Burke illustrates this two-way movement by considering the careers of words, for example, "create."

> "Create" apparently comes from an Indo-European root meaning simply "to make" and having such Greek derivatives as the words for "strength" and "accomplish" (*krato, kraino*). In theology, it comes to have the meaning of production as (in Coleridge's words) a dim analogue of Creation.

But the human origins of language are not for Burke an occasion for demystification. Burke is rather concerned with "the full scope of the resourcefulness of language."

[15] Kenneth Burke, *The Rhetoric of Religion* (Boston: Beacon Press, 1961), p. 7.

> Purpose will have its origins in bodily desires, most notably the appetites of food and sex. In this respect, it will be grounded in man's animality. But it will attain an immaterial counterpart in the principle of communication. Hence, purpose will have a secondary grounding in man's symbolicity. Add, next, the ways of empire that develop among the various societies of symbol-using animals and the conditions are set for their imagining of *love*, whether sacred or profane.[16]

Since language is rooted in personal experience and communal life, it does not become for Burke a system to be demystified as mechanical artifice. Burke's disposition is at once skeptical and constitutive.

Does this anti-constitutive impulse make deconstruction a nihilism? Deconstructionists deny that they are nihilists. Heidegger, whose work anticipates deconstruction in a number of ways, insisted on the positive function of what he calls de-struction. ". . . Destruction does not wish to bury the past in nullity; it has a positive intent."[17] And in his letter on humanism he addresses a series of ironic remarks toward those who regard any challenge to humanism as an act of nihilism.

> Because we are speaking against "humanism" people fear a defense of the inhuman and a glorification of barbaric brutality. For what is more "logical" than that for somebody who negates humanism nothing remains but the affirmation of inhumanity?
>
> Because we are speaking against "logic" people believe we are demanding that the rigor of thinking be renounced and in its place the arbitrariness of drives and feelings be installed and thus that "irrationalism" be pro-

[16] Ibid., p. 305.

[17] Martin Heidegger, *Basic Writings: From Being and Time to the Task of Thinking*, trans. Albert Hofstadter (New York: Harper & Row, 1976), p. 68.

> claimed as true. For what is more "logical" than that whoever speaks against the logical is defending the alogical?
>
> Because we are speaking against "values" people are horrified at a philosophy that ostensibly dares to despise humanity's best qualities. For what is more "logical" than that a thinking that denies values most necessarily pronounces everything valueless?[18]

Heidegger goes on to note that "being-in-the-world," "the death of god," and the speaking against "all that humanity deems high and holy" becomes for the pious humanist instances of an irresponsible and destructive "nihilism." There is a noteworthy hedge in Heidegger's irony. By enclosing words like logic and values in quotations marks, he is suggesting that the assault on the words is less radical than it seems. It is as if Heidegger means to reserve the possibility of these terms as positives for his own discourse—as if he wishes to define an authentic logic or value against what is deemed to be "logical" or "valuable." In which case, Heidegger's call for an "opening of vistas" may be seen as an attempt to propose a more convincing humanism against traditional "humanisms." If Heidegger hedges his critique, the deconstructionist in his most rigorous mood does not.

What Heidegger objects to in the humanist position is what he considers to be the subjectivity of values. ". . . It is important finally to realize that precisely through the characterization of something as 'a value' what is so valued is robbed of its worth. That is to say, by the assessment of something as a value what is valued is admitted only as an object for man's estimation."[19] It is Heidegger's project to free persons and things, so that they can be themselves. "Freedom, understood as letting beings be, is the fulfillment and consummation of the essence of truth in the sense of the disclosure of beings."[20] Subjectivity in whatever ver-

[18] Ibid., pp. 225-26.
[19] Ibid., p. 228.
[20] "On the Essence of Truth," in ibid., p. 129.

sion tends to appropriate its objects and deprive them of their full being. Heidegger's implicit value is a humanist value of freedom in plenitude, which he believes contemporary humanism effectively denies. Heidegger remains attached to the value terms of wholeness and plenitude in his use of the terms "disclosure" and "unconcealedness." Can the same be said for deconstruction? Are there substantial convincing positives in deconstructionist thought that would enable deconstructionists to assert Heidegger's ironies against misguided (naive) humanists?

An answer to the question might encompass structuralism and semiotics as well as deconstruction, for they all share hostility to "the idea of man." The perspective from which they study the behavior of man has led to the conclusion that the free person is a vain illusion. "The pleasure of revealing the culturally determined nature of behavior [writes Jonathan Culler] has doubtless been the impetus behind much semiotic analysis, but one would be mystified by the demystification itself if one thought that description of semiotic systems made the individual more free or that the semiotic analysis was in any way inspired by the prospect of liberating man."[21] What the semiotic, structuralist, and deconstructive analyses accomplish is a dissolution of the subject. "The goal of the human sciences," says Lévi-Strauss, "is not to constitute man but to dissolve him."[22] And Michel Foucault (neither a structuralist nor a deconstructionist, but a thinker on the same terrain) characterizes "man (as) only a recent invention, a figure not yet two centuries old, a simple fold in our knowledge that will soon disappear."[23] Derrida puts in question the assumptions on which the idea of man rests:

> The end of man (as a factual anthropological limit) is announced to thought from the vantage of the end of

[21] Jonathan Culler, *The Pursuit of Signs*, p. 32.
[22] Quoted in ibid., p. 32.
[23] Quoted in ibid., p. 33.

> man (as a determined opening or the infinity of a telos). Man is that which is in relation to his end, in the fundamentally equivocal sense of the word. Since always. The transcendental end can appear to itself and be unfolded only on the condition of mortality, of a relation to finitude as the origin of ideality. The name of man has always been inscribed in metaphysics between these two ends. It has meaning only in this eschato-teleological situation.[24]

There is an ambiguity in the idea of the disappearance of man or the disappearance of the idea of man that should make one hesitate in one's judgment of the prospect. Behind Foucault's remark is the Nietzschean idea of overcoming and surpassing. So nihilism is not necessarily the word for the prospect that man will disappear. Nevertheless, the prospect of the disappearance of the traditional idea of man (not man himself) is more real in post-structuralist discourse than any possible new creature that might ever emerge in the future, and it is the prospect of disappearance or dissolution that is being contemplated. Moreover, neither the dissolution nor any conceivable reconstitution of "man" is thought of as an exercise in freedom: it is rather the result of structuralist, semiotic, or deconstructive logic. Since the structuralist, the semiotician, and the deconstructionist propose their views in the interests of truth or a demystified state of affairs, it would be inadequate, if not irrelevant, simply to find these views undesirable because they are determined—unless, one wishes to claim, as I am claiming, that behind the "truth" is an exercise of subjective will, which does not have the force of impersonal necessity. In the case of the structuralist, the will is disposed toward the abstraction of structures; in the case of the deconstructionist toward unreachable abysses of emptiness.

[24] Jacques Derrida, *The Margins of Philosophy*, trans. Alan Bass (Chicago: University of Chicago Press, 1982), p. 123.

7

LITERATURE AS PLAY

So far we have addressed the cognitive rigor of deconstruction. What of its playfulness, which would seem to go counter to the ascetic direction of its rigor? The association of literature with play is hardly new. We need only invoke the self-delighting playfulness of Aristophanes and Shakespeare, among many others, to realize that the essence of comedy has always been play. Only a Puritan attitude within literature, which has affinities with a mistrust of literature itself, would want to banish self-delighting playfulness. The tradition of play in literature and in philosophical reflection about play has been strongly marked by theological or logocentric ideas. Deconstructive, or perhaps more broadly, post-modernist play is based on the evacuation of the logocentric ideas of plenitude, centrality, unity. So that the very idea of play has to be divided between rival meanings of the word.

With the birth and development of aesthetics as an intellectual discipline, play becomes a subject for serious, sometimes solemn, theoretical speculation. Perhaps the most extraordinary discourse on "the play impulse" in human life is Friedrich Schiller's *Letters on the Aesthetic Education of Man*, published in 1795 at the time of the Reign of Terror in France. (Schiller's work lies behind the later discussions of Johann Huizinga, Herbert Marcuse, and Norman O. Brown.) The date of publication is not fortuitous, for the letters are nothing less than an attempt to imagine a utopian alternative to the coercive society produced by the French Revolution. For Schiller it is in the aesthetic, not the political or moral, state that man fulfills his dream of happiness. By valuing the instincts as well as the intellect and the will, aesthetic man achieves the spontaneity and freedom of his full nature—its sensuous and material side and its intellectual or formal side. "He had learned to desire more nobly, so that he may not need to will sublimely." The actual failure of man to achieve the fullness of his nature is the consequence of a political misconception of the nature of man.

Though Schiller does not deny the intellectual or formal side of aesthetic life, he conceives it as a spontaneous result of the play impulse.

> The formal drive must not be the result of spiritual impotence or flabbiness of thought or will; for this would only degrade man. It must, if it is to be at all praiseworthy, spring from abundance of feeling and sensation. Sense herself must, with triumphant power, remain mistress of her own domain, and resist the violence which the mind, by its usurping tactics, would fain inflict upon her. In a single word: Personality must keep the sensuous drive within its proper bounds and receptivity, or Nature, must do the same with the formal drive.

Schiller cannot entirely avoid the language of power in his conception of spontaneous play. Sense must assert itself with *triumphant power*, it must *resist* the usurping tactics of mind and the sensuous drive must be *kept in bounds*. But for Schiller this restraint enhances the play impulse. It is, so to speak, the guarantee of its seriousness. Play, for Schiller, is an end in itself, possessing no purpose beyond the enjoyment it offers. And the enjoyment is conveyed in the words pleasure, freedom, nobility.

> The things he possesses, the things he produces, may no longer bear upon them the marks of their use. . . . Disinterested and undirected pleasure is now numbered among the necessities of existence, and what is in fact

> unnecessary soon becomes the best part of his delight. . . . In the Aesthetic State everything—even the tool which serves—is a free citizen, having equal rights with the noblest, and the mind, which would force the patient mass beneath the yoke of its purposes, must here obtain its consent.

But how does man achieve the aesthetic condition? Here Schiller invokes the idea or metaphor of organic development against any revolutionary project that disrupts the living process. In *Culture and the Radical Conscience*, I noted that "though [Schiller's] argument seems to be an early version of the psychology of liberation fostered by Marcuse and Brown and though it has democratic ambitions, it is distinguished by its refusal to identify in a revolutionary way the need for liberation with the assertion that liberation is at hand. 'Liberation' has to be nurtured like a plant, to use an organic simile that would have suited Schiller."[1]

In the nineteenth and early twentieth centuries, discussions of play are bound by organic metaphors in which plenitude, spontaneity, and unity are implicitly or explicitly expressed. A character in a dialogue of Georg Lukács (written early in his career) gives a suggestive account of play as a fruitfully disturbing proliferation of energy within the fullness and unity of life.

> To break up the unity simply so as to make it felt still more strongly—to make the unity felt at the same time as the things which are destroying it! to be able to play: that is the only true sovereignty. We play with things, but we remain the same and the things stay as they were. But both have been enhanced during the game and through the game. Lawrence Sterne plays, always, all the time, with the gravest notions of man and destiny. And his characters and their destinies acquire incredible grav-

[1] *Culture and the Radical Conscience* (Cambridge, Mass.: Harvard University Press, 1973), pp. 125-32.

> ity through the fact that all his playing doesn't really shift them from the spot where they stand, it just washes against them like the sea against a cliff, yet the cliff stands firm in the play of waves, and the more violently the waves break against them from all sides, the more we sense the cliff's solidity. And yet he is only playing with them. It is only his playful will that gives him this gravity.[2]

The adversary in the debate wonders whether the reason for play in Sterne's work is an "inability to control his exuberant strength, or . . . a coverup for weakness?" Both characters in the dialogue share an organic vision of life, so that neither of them entertains the possibility of the simultaneous existence of two kinds of play, one whose "exuberant strength" expresses the fullness of life and the other whose energy dissembles emptiness.

Organicism has been suspect as a freedom-denying determinism. "To substitute the concept of growth [writes Meyer Abrams] for the operation of a mechanism in the psychology of invention seems merely to exchange one kind of determinism for another, while to replace the mental artisan planner by the concept of organic self-generation makes it difficult, analogically, to justify the participation of consciousness in the creative process."[3] In his gloss on this passage, Jonathan Culler puts the case in terms of freedom. "Organicist language was introduced in order to distinguish the servile and combinatory operations of fancy from the creativity and freedom of the Imagination, but this representation of freedom ends by denying the freedom it was supposed to represent."[4] The organicist might respond that freedom means vital power, the capacity to

[2] "Richness, Chaos, and Form," in *Soul and Form*, trans. Anna Bostock (Cambridge, Mass.: MIT Press, 1974, 1978), pp. 137-38.

[3] M. H. Abrams, *The Mirror and The Lamp* (New York: Oxford University Press, 1953), p. 158.

[4] Jonathan Culler, *The Pursuit of Signs* (Ithaca, N.Y.: Cornell University Press, 1981), p. 158.

enact the laws of one's being. The experience of freedom is consonant with the experience of necessity. To be sure, tyrants have justified their tyranny by asserting the congruence of freedom and necessity. But psychologically, one's sense of power and freedom depends on the feeling that one is enacting the inner necessity of one's nature. It should be noted that the same ambiguities of freedom and necessity that inhere in the idea of teleology inhere in the idea of organic form. In any event, the deconstructive argument against organicism is not conducted in behalf of an idea of freedom, since in the deconstructive perspective freedom is an illusion.

In the organicist view, "exuberant" strength is at once a given and a goal. Each individual avails himself of the plenitude of a life that is the ground of his existence; at the same time, he aspires to a richer and more complete life. Plenitude assumes the possible completeness of the subject as a goal, since it is never the case in actual experience. Completeness is achieved through a process that occurs in time. Beginnings, middles, and endings are essential to the organic process. Completeness may circumscribe a subject, but such completeness in the organic view tends to be provisional, for it implies the discreteness and separateness of things that contradict the organic ambition for greater and greater wholeness. In *Natural Supernaturalism*, Meyer Abrams claims that "what was distinctive in Romantic thought was the normative emphasis not so much on plenitude as such, but on an organized unity in which all individuation and diversity survive, in Coleridge's terms, as distinction without division."[5] And yet Abrams's subsequent exposition of romantic doctrine makes clear that the unity of the cosmos could not be encompassed by the finite human mind. According to Fichte, whose view is characteristic, "the ultimate goal of man . . . is utterly unattainable . . . his way to it must

[5] M. H. Abrams, *Natural Supernaturalism* (New York: W. W. Norton, 1971), p. 185.

be endless."[6] The journey or the activity becomes an end in itself. This at least is the case for imaginative literature. Hegel claims for philosophy (his philosophy) the ability to encompass the whole. "The truth is not rationally grasped, or 'comprehended,' however, until the final stage, the achievement of genuine philosophy, which supersedes, while preserving its substance, the image-making of revealed religion," and, one might add, of poetic vision.[7] If the romantics do not attain unity, they nevertheless retain it as a goal.

The "logic" of organicism is the view of life as a seamless continuity. The boundaries of things, which make for parts, forms, and fragments, have only provisional interest. They do not add up to life itself. The sum is always greater than the parts, an organicist fact, which makes mathematics an alien metaphorical system. Life in its fullness remains beyond the finitizing capabilities of language, which can only suggest its fullness and depth. "We murder to dissect": the metaphor of the laboratory applies to language, that is, to any finitizing or mechanistic activity that fails to respect the wholeness, the seamlessness, and fullness of life itself. The despair of the romantic poet comes from his conviction of both the inadequacy and the necessity of language. The obverse of the organicist view of wholeness may be a kind of death, an unwillingness to credit the existence of the manifest forms of life. Death may be the delicious promise of release or it may cause terror at the prospect of the abyss. Emptiness is the shadow of organic plenitude. The organicist view does not deny the existence of fragmentation, discontinuity, opposition. It knows that the transgressive and disruptive impulse is present in every strong imagination. What the organicist view rejects is the assumption that discontinuity and opposition are prior to unity and harmony. "There can be no reconciliation," Ste-

[6] Quoted in ibid., p. 216.

[7] Ibid., p. 233.

phen Dedalus remarks in *Ulysses*, "if there has not been a sundering." Neither can there be a sundering where there has not been a unity. Where there has been sundering there has been wholeness and there may be healing, reconciliation, and restoration to wholeness. Playfulness, in the organicist view, becomes a paradoxical expression of unity. What is at the center is so strong and alive that the prodigality and proliferation that it generates neither displaces nor diminishes the unity. Thus the characters and destiny of Lawrence Sterne's characters "acquire incredible gravity through the fact that all his playing doesn't really shift them from the spot where they stand. . . ."

The habit of employing the terms play and game interchangeably conceals an important difference in the implications of the words. Games are always rule-bound, a condition that deprives the "playing" of them of a certain spontaneity. When a player has sufficiently internalized the rules, he may take them for granted and play with a freedom and abandon that seems to ignore the rules. However, so long as he plays the game he cannot violate the rules. Play, on the other hand, does not always seem to be confined to rules, filled as it is with improvisation. The distinction may be illusory in the sense that the abandon of the player may conceal rules that determine even the improvisations, and the rule-bound character of the game may be seen simply as the condition for the freedom of play. But the words do stress the opposite or different sides of the playing or gaming activity—and it is important to keep the distinction in mind.

In considering what the play of language has come to mean in contemporary literary discourse, one should begin with the rule-bound character of the game. In *Homo Ludens*, Johann Huizinga stresses the rules of the game, which, in his view, are a stay against the chaos of "real life." Huizinga cites Paul Valéry's remark: "No skepticism is possible where the rules of a game are concerned, for the principle underlying them is an unshakeable faith." Valéry might have said more accurately that when skepticism appears the rules of the game are in jeopardy, for he also observes that "if the rules are transgressed the whole play-world collapses. The game is over. The umpire's whistle breaks the spell and sets 'real' life going again."[8] The introduction of the terms skepticism and faith immediately dispels any frivolous association that attaches to the idea of play. Play, in this view, is an originating energy of culture. It is the expression of a sacred ritual, having no purpose beyond itself, not because it is frivolous, but because it is a fulfillment of human life. "Play consecrated to the Deity, the highest goal of man's endeavor—such was Plato's conception of religion," according to Huizinga.[9]

If we revise Valéry's formulation and ask what are the conditions under which the rules of the game are immune from skepticism, the answer, I think, is that the game is not threatened when the player has a conviction of the fullness of life, that is, when life itself is not experienced as a *mere* game. An overflowing play that expresses the fullness of life is the freedom beyond the rules of the game. When that conviction disappears the game ceases to be an occasion for personal expression, it becomes instead a mechanism to be disassembled and examined with detachment. If our relation to life and the games becomes severely problematic, our focus is displaced from the playing of the game to the arbitrariness that initiates the constellation of rules that constitute the game.

It is this displacement of focus that characterizes the deconstructive theory and practice of play. The displacement (or the consciousness of it) did not, however, originate with deconstruction. It can be found in the fiction, for example, of Samuel Beckett, whose *Endgame* makes the displacement transparent.

[8] *Homo Ludens* (Boston: Beacon Press, 1955), p. 27.

[9] Ibid., p. 11.

HAMM: We're beginning to . . . to . . . mean something?
CLOV: Mean something. You and I, mean something! (Brief laugh.) Ah That's a good one!
HAMM: I wonder. (Pause) Imagine if a rational being came back to earth, wouldn't he be able to get ideas into his head if he observed us long enough.

Storytelling in Beckett's trilogy (*Molloy, Malone Dies,* and *The Unnameable*) is a kind of playing in order to fill the void of the self, but it is unsuccessful playing, since the void continually exposes the fiction. A story assumes or invents a self that can never achieve *being* or *meaning* (coextensive terms in Beckett's world). Beckett gives us not so much a fiction as an ontology of fiction, voices that continually question their own existences.

> Of myself I could never tell, any more than live or tell of others. How could I have, who never tried? To show myself now, on the point of vanishing, at the same time as the stranger, and by the same grace, that would be no ordinary last straw.

The self in Beckett's world is a Cartesian machine that has either broken down or has never quite been constructed. Its indeterminacy is not to be confused with a being for whom there is always the potentiality of a fuller realization. There is an odd conjunction of creativity and impotence in Beckett's imagination with the implication that the condition of nonbeing and meaninglessness is universal and insurmountable. Beckett does not project his world as the production of a particular imagination or temperament. It is rather revealed to us as a discovery of the nature of things. Such a world can be filled only by language, which must always be suspect, since it is without conviction or reference—or it may be said to have the conviction of suspicion and the referentiality of chaos and emptiness.

What remains irreducible in Beckett's work, however, is

the fact that he writes plays and novels. Robbe-Grillet has remarked apropos of Beckett's plays that the theater implies "a metaphysics of presence," presence meaning thereness (*être-là*) without signification. Robbe-Grillet quotes Heidegger: "The human condition . . . is to be there." In *Waiting for Godot*, Gogo and Didi are men, they are on stage, they are there. This is perhaps all that can be said about or for them. The course of the play, to be sure, is disintegration. "The hero of Beckett's narrative [Robbe-Grillet writes] deteriorates from book to book, faster and faster. Feeble, but still capable of travelling on a bicycle he rapidly loses the use of his limbs . . . finds himself imprisoned in a room . . . his senses gradually abandon him." Yet, as Robbe-Grillet notes, the character continues to wear garters. Robbe-Grillet formulates the paradox of his thereness. In spite of the thereness: "What little has been given to us from the start—which seemed to be nothing—is soon corrupted before our eyes . . . to a less than nothing." (Pozzo is deprived of sight, Lucky of speech.) Thereness is compatible with nothing, because thereness is value-neutral, devoid of meaning or signification.

Thereness in Robbe-Grillet's sense (it is not Beckett's) is a negative condition that cannot be escaped; consequently any freedom that Beckett's characters have may be illusory. "They have nothing to recite . . . to invent . . . they must remain because they are waiting for Godot." Robbe-Grillet's account of Beckett's work leads to a criticism of what he regards as Beckett's mistaken attempt to recuperate meaning through the tragic sense of the loss of meaning. Robbe-Grillet wrote his article on Beckett at a time (1957) when he was developing a phenomenology of a value-free presence, which would disable the tragic longing for significance. But Robbe-Grillet's phenomenology and critique depends upon an arbitrary division between presence and meaning, which he may be imposing upon Beckett. Barthes has incisively pointed out in an essay on Robbe-Grillet that Robbe-Grillet's attempt to achieve a neutral (objective) whiteness of presentation, is willy-nilly an expression of his own subjectivity. The act of signification, even if it is hostile to the idea of signification, is inescapable.[10]

If, as Raymond Federman says, Beckett's "fiction no longer relates a story (past realities reshaped by the process of imagination into an artistic form), but it simply reflects upon itself, upon its own chaotic verbal process, that is to say upon its own (defective) substance—language,"[11] how or why does Beckett continue to write? The question is not addressed to Beckett's biography but to the "logic" of his writing. The answer depends, I think, on a distinction between two senses of the defectiveness of language. Language can betray meaning (i.e., propositional sense) through sheer personal incompetence, or in exploring the possible resources of language, it can reveal the intrinsic defectiveness of language in which one always glimpses meaning. It is tempting to attribute the second sense of the defectiveness of language to Beckett's work. One might say that he brings language as close as possible to propositional and referential sense, and when his language falls back into verbal chaos it is because language is intrinsically incapable of achieving the intelligibility it desires. Such a view is in keeping with an implication of his work that I noted above: Beckett has discovered a universal condition; he gives us a view of the nature of things. (The epistemology underlying this view

[10] See Bruce Morrisette, "Robbe-Grillet as a Critic of Samuel Beckett," in *Samuel Beckett Now*, ed. Melvin Friedman (Chicago: University of Chicago Press, 1970), pp. 59ff. For Jacques Derrida the absence of meaning is a condition of play, to which the seriousness of meaning is opposed. "Only the serious has a *meaning*: play, which no longer has one, is serious only to the extent to which 'the absence of meaning is also a meaning.' . . . The seriousness of death and pain is the servility of thought." *Writing and Difference*, trans. Alan Bass (Chicago: University of Chicago Press, 1978), p. 335. For his discussion of Robbe-Grillet, see Roland Barthes's "Last Word on Robbe-Grillet" in *Critical Essays*, trans. Richard Howard (Evanston, Ill.: Northwestern University Press, 1972), pp. 197-204.

[11] "Beckettian Paradox: Who is Telling the Truth?" in *Samuel Beckett Now*, p. 112.

is graphically expressed by Georgias of L. who, according to A. J. Leventhal, propounded the following theorems:

1. Nothing is.
2. If anything is, it cannot be known.
3. If anything is, and cannot be known, it cannot be expressed in speech.[12]

And yet (and here is the particular relevance of Beckett) only speech or writing can express this sequence. But the language after all is that of Beckett and his characters whose deficiencies are particular, so that the element of sheer personal incompetence enters in—not so much the incompetence of language as the language of an incompetent person. This view of Beckett is confirmed by a hope expressed in *Texts for Nothing*: "And yet I have high hopes, I give you my word, high hopes, that one day I may tell a story, yet another, with me, kinds of men as in the days when I played all regardless or nearly, worked and played." The effectiveness of story and language depends on the character and quality of persons. It is not intrinsic to the machinery of language. Beckett's work equivocates, I think, between the two senses (intrinsic and personal) of the defectiveness of language.[13]

Beckett's characters perform the act of storytelling under the conditions of suspicion. Like the writer, they are bemused by the activity, at once dismissive of the enterprise and protective of it as the only enterprise possible. In this spirit of self-mistrust, Donald Barthelme reflects upon the conditions of writing that no longer refers to an external reality: "Another story about writing a story? Another regressus in infinitum? Who doesn't prefer art that at least

[12] Quoted in Rosette Lamont, "Beckett's Metaphysics of Choiceless Awareness," ibid., p. 201.

[13] Olga Bernal writes of Beckett as one might write of deconstruction: "This is not the first time in the history of literature that language no longer situates itself opposite the world, but opposite itself." "L'Oubli des Noms," *Le Monde*, 17 Jan. 1968.

overtly imitates something other than its own processes? That doesn't continually proclaim 'Don't forget I'm an artifice!' " Barthelme writes stories that do not forget that they are artifices, because they are the only stories that he can tell. However, Barthelme does not say that they are the only stories that can be told. In a similar spirit John Barth writes: "How does one write a novella? How find the channel, bewildered in these creeks and crannies? Storytelling isn't my cup of wine? isn't somebody's; my plot doesn't rise and fall in meaningful stages but . . . digresses, retreats, hesitates, groans from its utter et cetera, collapses, dies."

Skepticism about the possibility of telling stories about the "real" world may erode the sense of reality, but it does not extinguish the vocabulary that represents it. Traces of reality survive in language itself. Reality, society, self, pleasure, pain are terms that are taken into the most skeptical kind of discourse as part of its necessity. The writer's reluctance may be registered by quotation marks or by a distancing reflectiveness which raises continuous doubt about the adequacy of the very terms of discourse. No writer can perform this task adequately, because adequacy would produce the written equivalent of stammering and finally silence. The result, then, in varying degrees, is a plural or even confused discourse of shifting and contending vocabularies offering multiple perspectives, an infinitely regressive and playful interrogation of the premises of discourse.

The deconstructive view, insisting on the insurmountable gap between word and thing, conceives of all discourse as a "field of infinite substitutions in the closure of a finite ensemble," and, one should add, free of notions of coherence and unity. The liberation from the definitiveness of reference goes hand in hand with a liberation from the imperative of coherence. The fertility of language in generating multiple meaning establishes, in the view of deconstruction, the priority of equivocal readings over univocal readings. Having banished the constraints of voice and will, deconstruction sanctions the richest possible play of "meaning," or rather the absence of meaning. If "we are the product rather than the agent of language,"[14] as de Man says, we engage in an exercise in futility in trying to constrain the activity of language through voice and will. Like a game, language has its rules, its mechanism, and the game plays itself. The playing is not in any way determined by the will of the player.

This view of discursive play is contrasted with a structuralist view, which has its source in a romantic belief in presence. Derrida characterizes the structuralist view in the following manner. "The center also closes off the play which it opens up and makes possible. . . . The concept of centered structure is in fact the concept of a play based on a fundamental ground, a play constituted on the basis of a fundamental immobility and a reassuring attitude, which itself is beyond the realm of play. . . . (The) matrix (of history of the concept of structure) is the determination of Being as *presence* in all senses of the word."[15] As Frank Lentricchia remarks, "unlike Kant, Derrida speaks not of a free-play in the world, but a 'free-play of the world.' "[16] (Free play is sheer arbitrariness; if it is in the world, the arbitrariness does not define the world, if of the world, it of course does.) The game of discourse may be threatened in a perspective of floating signifiers (the extreme reduction of the fact that "language and meaning do not coincide"),[17]

[14] "Shelley Disfigured," in *Deconstruction and Criticism*, ed. Harold Bloom (New York: The Seabury Press, 1979), p. 68.

[15] Jacques Derrida, "Structure, Sign and Play," in *Writing and Difference*, p. 279.

[16] *After the New Criticism* (Chicago: University of Chicago Press, 1980), p. 168.

[17] Note, on the deconstructionist view, the absence of coincidence between language and meaning is radical—unlike the view of the speech-act theorist: "A Speaker may mean more than what he actually says, but it is always in principle possible for him to say exactly what he means." Searle, *Speech Acts: An Essay in the Philosophy of Language* (Cambridge and New York: Cambridge University Press, 1969), p. 18.

gratuitous verbal behavior that no longer wishes to enclose itself in its own coherence, though it might find itself impelled to do so by an unmastered need for order.

Paul de Man envisages the possibility of chaos in both life and discourse, "the possibility . . . that the entire construction of drives, substitutions, and representations is the aberrant, metaphysical correlative of the absolute randomness of language prior to any figuration of meaning."[18] If this is so, the game of discourse is a stubborn and incorrigible refusal to allow the "truth" of randomness to prevail. De Man writes elsewhere:

> And to read is to understand, to question, to know, to forget, to erase, to deface, to repeat—that is to say, the endless prosopopoeia by which the dead are made to have a face and a voice which tells the allegory of their demise and allows us to apostrophize them in our turn. No degree of knowledge can ever stop this madness, for it is the madness of words. What would be naive is to believe that this strategy, which is not our strategy as subjects, since we are its product rather than its agent, can be a source of value and has to be celebrated or denounced accordingly.[19]

The demystifying or deconstructive process cannot by itself undo the game of discourse, much as it tries, for as de Man realistically notes: "no degree of knowledge can ever stop this madness, for it is the madness of words." Such a view inverts the normal or naive hierarchy of reason and sanity. To live, to speak, to write, to read is madness; sanity is the unrelenting knowledge of our nothingness. No degree of knowledge can stop the madness, because such knowledge fully lived would be suicide. De Man takes us beyond skepticism to a vision of discursive futility.

[18] Quoted in Harold Bloom, "The Breaking of Form" in *Deconstruction and Criticism*, p. 4.

[19] Paul de Man, "Shelley Disfigured," in ibid., p. 68.

Skepticism need not be a disabling attitude. The skeptic may take pleasure in the uncertainties of knowing reality. In a famous statement about the Negative Capability, John Keats proposed uncertainty and doubt as a capacity, indeed the greatest capacity of the literary imagination. The Negative Capability occurs in a "man . . . capable of being in uncertainties, mysteries, doubts without any irritable reaching after fact and reason." This negative condition is not the void, for the poet has gained a freedom to participate as variously as possible in the plenitude of being. In a letter Keats writes: "What the imagination seizes as beauty must be truth . . . the imagination may be compared to Adam's dream—he awoke and found it truth." Only the philosopher who has reached the still center may have a fuller experience of plenitude. Keats's Negative Capability links uncertainty and plenitude. In a Keatsian spirit, Kenneth Burke speaks of characters possessing "*degrees of being* in proportion to the variety of perspectives from which they can with justice be perceived."[20] "Reality," Nabokov notes in his Afterword to *Lolita*, "is one of the few words which mean nothing without quotes." But for Nabokov there is no reason to despair. The imaginative skeptic learns to play with his uncertainties, to turn them into endlessly amusing and deeply serious games. The imagination may grow so bold that it overcomes reality, and skepticism loses its doubt.

The conviction of plenitude is, of course, not susceptible to proof, but neither is the conviction of emptiness. Emptiness or nothingness is a cultural category that might require the kind of "proof" expected for the claim of plenitude. In adjudicating between deconstruction and organicism, we are dealing more with temperament and disposition and its historical determinants than with logic and evidence.

Even among deconstructionists one notices differences

[20] *A Grammar of Motives* (Berkeley and Los Angeles: University of California Press, 1969), p. 504.

of temperament (and history) reflected in the particular doctrine of deconstruction being asserted. Thus Hillis Miller with his residual humanism values the fertility of the method. "The hypothesis of a possible heterogeneity in literary texts is more flexible, more open to a given work, than the assumption that a good work of literature is necessarily going to be 'organically unified.' " Good liberal that he is, Miller sees deconstruction as an attempt "to resist the totalizing and totalitarian tendencies of criticism."[21] Unlike de Man, he is not so much interested in "truth" as in its pragmatic usefulness ("it works"). And again unlike de Man, he values its pluralism, not its claim to mastery over the work. De Man may be truer to the austere, ascetic spirit of deconstruction. Miller's domestication of it weakens its grip.

In any event, in distinguishing between de Man and Miller as I am doing, I am of course "listening" to the differences with which their voices banish voice. I am assuming in de Man a rigorous will to discover disorder and emptiness and in Miller a will to discover diversity and richness. I am also assuming that language does not alone decide whether meaning is stable or unstable; it is the subject or user of language who decides what he wishes to mean or do with language, according to his temperament, his talents and the circumstances in which he finds himself, though what he means or does may have implications beyond what he intends.

Whether or not de Man's version represents the "true" spirit of deconstruction, its insistence on rigor (shared in varying degrees by Derrida, Miller, and other deconstructionists) restricts the *freedom* of deconstructive play. In its sensitivity to the repressiveness of the binding, continuous element in organic form, deconstruction would seem to have liberationist implications. In proposing the provisionality of the mechanical model, deconstruction is declaring

[21] J. H. Miller, "The Critic as Host," in *Deconstruction and Criticism*, p. 252.

its freedom to disassemble the mechanical "unity," altering the relations of parts to one another without altering the machine. And yet its mistrust of plenitude and spontaneity justifies the repressive image that Geoffrey Hartman applies to them: "boa deconstructors."[22] Frank Lentricchia is mistaken in characterizing the "drift of post-structuralism" in the following manner. "The shift from cognitive terms ('wrong,' 'valid') to ethical and practical language ('good,' 'interesting') is entirely consistent with the drift of American post-structuralism (freedom, joy, affirmation, the erotic pleasure of the text) and especially harmonious with de Man's Nietzschean bias."[23] As I show in my discussion of *Allegories of Reading*, de Man divides Nietzsche between his austere deconstructive side and his "demagogic," vitalist, affirmative side and values the first at the expense of the second. Freedom, joy, affirmation are sentimental terms, obvious targets for deconstructive skepticism. Deconstructive playfulness is strongly modified by the ascetic strain that determines its cognitive rigor.

[22] Ibid., p. ix.

[23] *After the New Criticism*, p. 185.

CONCLUSION: DECONSTRUCTION AND SOCIAL CRITICISM

The implications of deconstruction extend beyond texts. One potential casualty of deconstruction is social criticism. Deconstruction makes social criticism of whatever inspiration (literary, historical, philosophical) very difficult, if not impossible. The touchstone for a literary-inspired social criticism has been of course, Matthew Arnold. Arnold had an abundant capacity for doubt, but he assumed the presence and fullness of the cultural tradition. Disinterestedness, the free play of the mind upon our "stock habits of thought and feeling" never really extended to the touchstones that formed his convictions. Arnold's particular touchstones are, of course, vulnerable to criticism. The Hebraistic or puritanical constraints of his thought are unnecessarily exclusionary, if they disable us from fully appreciating the comic play of Chaucer's imagination or of Keats's sensuousness. But Arnold's Hellenism, like Keats's Negative Capability, represents, in principle at least, a link between imaginative and intellectual play and plenitude necessary to an evaluative social and literary criticism. It is a link that contemporary skepticism has severed at great cost. The imagination can no longer play its games with confidence, for the deepest knowledge of the critic is of the vacuity on which those games rest. Even the rules of the game are not immune to skepticism. All the traditional discriminations between the genuine and false uses of language, which have given social criticism (the work of Arnold and Orwell, for instance) a certain power, is denied by deconstruction as unearned and inauthentic.

There are signs of dissatisfaction even among post-structuralist critics who wish to restore the text and the critical act to the world. Edward Said, for all his respect for Derrida and de Man, wants criticism to become a (left) radical presence in politics and society.[1] Invoking Marx and Foucault against deconstruction, particularly in the version represented by de Man, Frank Lentricchia, in a more aggressive spirit than Said's, characterizes "the political fruit" of "the bottomless self-irony" of de Man as "not caution and care (good qualities for the active intellectual) but timidity, indifference, and impotence—qualities which pass in the academy in the guise of sophistication and wisdom."[2]

Such criticism, coming from a "traditional" humanist would doubtless be dismissed as a kind of demagogy, the sort of rhetoric that would itself be vulnerable to deconstructive rigor. However, coming from the left, even a rhetorical criticism has a certain privilege with a deconstructionist like Derrida because of his connections with, if not roots in, the French left. So Derrida responds to questions about the political efficacy of deconstruction (in *Positions*) by implying the radical or subversive nature of putting everything in question. As evidence of his radicalism, he can adduce the very movement of his thought, which seeks to reverse the hierarchy of domination of every binary opposition (e.g., man-woman).

> To deconstruct the opposition, first of all, is to overturn the hierarchy at a given moment. To overlook the phase of overturning is to forget the conflictual and subordinating structure of oppositions. Therefore one might proceed too quickly to a *neutralization* that *in practice* would leave the previous field untouched, leaving one no hold on the previous opposition, thereby preventing any means of *intervening* in the field effectively. We know what al-

[1] See Edward Said, *The World, The Text, The Critic* (Cambridge, Mass.: Harvard University Press, 1983).

[2] Frank Lentricchia, "Foucault," *Raritan* 2 (Summer 1982), 57-58.

> ways have been the *practical* (particularly *political*) effects of immediately jumping *beyond* oppositions, and of protests in the simple form of *neither* this *nor* that.[3]

Derrida is doing little more here than describing what in fact does happen in the first phase of revolutionary insurgency, when one injustice resentfully replaces another. It is not at all clear, however, why the logic of deconstruction dictates such a reversal. Derrida's interviews in *Positions* read like attempts to reconcile in some degree the autonomous movement of his thought with the conventional politics of the left.[4] Of course, a deconstructionist like de Man, free of anxiety about his political credentials (whatever they may be), may choose to resist the pragmatic challenge and refuse to compromise the cognitive integrity of his enterprise. So long as its rigor remains persuasive, he can dismiss his critics of whatever political orientation as irrelevant ideologues.

The challenge from the left, however, is symptomatic of what is felt to be radical limitation in the deconstructive "ethic." As I have tried to show, the inadequacy of deconstructive skepticism is to be found in its intrinsic inability to deal with the question of values and, in particular, of its own values. Any activity, including the activity of deconstructing all activities, is founded on interests and values that constitute the origins of the activity. To say this is not

[3] *Positions*, trans. Alan Bass (Chicago: University of Chicago Press, 1981), p. 41.

[4] Jonathan Culler, a recent advocate of deconstruction, seems even more eager than Derrida to establish the progressive credentials of deconstuction. In responding to Michael Ryan's effort to harness deconstruction to Marxism, Jonathan Culler asks rhetorically whether one needs "Derrida to unravel the contradictions of right-wing political rhetoric" (*On Deconstruction: Theory and Practice after Structuralism* (Ithaca, N.Y.: Cornell University Press, 1982), p. 158. Culler would like to save Derrida for more interesting questions about "what is truly progressive or not." Culler does not raise a question about left-wing rhetoric. Apparently it is off limits, a case of Deconstruction Limited.

to endorse any particular activity, whether it be Marxist, Foucauldian, Derridean, or Arnoldian, but it is to redefine the nature of the debate, which has implicitly privileged the skeptical mode. The redefinition of the debate would permit us to reexamine assumptions and views that have been discredited as naive in the skeptical perspective.

The values and interests that determine discourse (in its possible variety) emerge from a combination of character (temperament, disposition) and history (circumstance, experience). History has been traditionally allied to relativism. Roland Barthes, for example, invokes history in order to relativize nature, which in modern thought has tended to perform the role of an eternal verity. But history has its own way of privileging events, of constructing patterns of significance, which exclude or dismiss other events and patterns. The authority-conferring, teleologizing tendency of history is put forcefully, if negatively, by Stephen Dedalus in *Ulysses*:

> time has branded events and fettered they are lodged in the infinite possibilities they have ousted. But can those have been possible seeing that they never were? Or was that only possible which came to pass?

The events that occur, the pattern or patterns that they make, suggest at any moment needs, desires, and values. One philosophical "metaphor" for this activity of privileging and exclusion is historical determinism. A need or value may become an imperative to act or to speak in a particular way. What the metaphor expresses in an unnecessarily constricted form (human beings may, after all, originate history) is the truth that not everything is possible: that the very activity of privileging is part of real historical life.

In moments of uncertainty (which may indeed be frequent), we may experience the correlative of the philosophical condition in which these motives develop. Uncertainty or skepticism need not be the perspective from which we view all the seasons of our lives or the texts that occupy our lives. What is missing from the radically skeptical view of privilege is a historical sense of the conditions under which certain views emerge and are felt to have authority, including the skeptical view.

I cannot pretend to offer a sociological analysis of our present moral and political situation, but it seems evident to me that we live in a time when most reflective people have a sense of the inadequacy of the available choices. Neither liberalism nor conservatism, socialism nor capitalism (one can list other such oppositions) can galvanize intellect and will, because of a sensed vulnerability of all positions. All that the lucid intelligence can do is turn back upon itself and trace the lines of its activity. It is inconceivable (at least to me) that a deconstructive attitude could exist in the time of the Spanish Civil War, World War II, or in Solzhenitsyn's Soviet Union. This is not to say that the skeptical intelligence could not direct a stream of fresh (even satiric) thought on the clichés that supported the Loyalist cause in Spain (see Orwell's *Homage to Catalonia*) or the Allied war effort or on Russian dissident thought. It is simply that skepticism never fully defined such an intelligence, that it remained rooted in convictions about truth, decency, and humanity, terms that it had no interest in deconstructing. Indeed, its concern is with the moments when truth, decency, and humanity are betrayed by the right side. It should be clear that I am speaking not of literary criticism or theory exclusively but of imaginative literature and politics as well.

The limitations, if not misdirection, of the deconstructionist project can perhaps be illustrated by a consideration of a particular passage from an essay by Allen Tate. The passage is from the essay "The Man of Letters in the Modern World" and it is an expression of what might be called the sensibility of the cultivated man in a democratic society, who fears the debasement of the values of a free society in a degenerate linguistic tendency in democracy itself. It is a useful passage for our purposes because it typifies a widely shared sensibility and would seem to be an easy target for deconstruction.

> It is a tragedy of contemporary society that so much of democratic theory reaches us in the language of "drive," "stimulus," and "response." This is not the language of freemen, it is the language of slaves. The language of freemen substitutes for these words, respectively, *end, choice,* and *discrimination.* Here are two sets of analogies, the one subrational and servile, the other rational and free.[5]

What might a healthy skepticism say in response to a disabling deconstructionist suspicion of *freedom, end, choice,* and *discrimination*?

A person believing in the values of freedom and rationality could dispute Tate's view. He might point out that the positing of an end might eliminate or diminish alternatives, thus strongly qualifying the sense of freedom. He might find in the making of discriminations a threat to the freedom of those being discriminated against or to the alternatives dismissed by the discrimination. He might similarly scrutinize the words stimulus, response, and drive and find that in certain circumstances they need not constitute a threat to reason or freedom. But whatever the character of the dispute, there would be a common ground in the acceptance of the value of rationality and freedom.

It could be objected that the existence of diametrically opposed views on freedom (for example: "freedom is the recognition of necessity" versus "freedom is the escape from or transcendence of necessity") evacuates the term of substantial content and therefore requires the rigor of semiotic or deconstructive scrutiny. To this objection one could convincingly reply that the very need for the both sides to appeal to the idea of freedom means that the term evokes

[5] Allen Tate, *Essays of Four Decades* (Chicago: The Swallow Press, 1968), p. 12.

an experience or a feeling that most people (if not everyone) regard as valuable or essential to life. Skeptical scrutiny may come to rest in a clarification of values that may be immune to endless deconstruction.

There may be something purgative in the deconstructive process, in the endlessly regressive self-interrogation that enables us to see the difficulties in any position we might take. But it would be delusive to think that such an activity as an end in itself does not risk the frivolity of a mere game or that it can satisfy needs to which a criticism of conviction and commitment is addressed. (It is a question whether it can even satisfy "the play impulse," which animates an aesthetic of plenitude.) Though one cannot simply will "engaged" criticism into existence, a combination of will and changed historical circumstances in the future will doubtless bring it about, and it will be criticism of more than one ideological persuasion.

In resisting the identification of radical skepticism with criticism itself, I do not want to disqualify it as a possible type of criticism. I can even imagine a skeptic of the radical sort agreeing with the limits I am placing on skepticism. What I object to is a dogmatism that conceives plenitude or emptiness, wholeness, or fragmentation, teleology or randomness as metaphysical priorities rather then alternative possibilities for different consciousnesses, or even within a single consciousness. If I choose to challenge the current prestige of skepticism (a skepticism in some cases verging on nihilism), it is not to deny its validity altogether. Skepticism is an historically conditioned view of experience, which does not disqualify it as a method or a system of thought, but its historical character should bar it from putting on metaphysical or universalistic airs. Certainly in the hands of epigoni and graduate students who possess neither the experience nor the conviction of deconstructive skepticism, deconstruction may become an absurd and wholly unjustified mechanical exercise. In studying the new skepticism in literary theory and criticism, I have tried to hear its voice (as a possible voice among other voices), judge its logic, understand its historical determination. The terms of skeptical theory (whatever the version) are the terms not of an impersonal metaphysics, but of the subject's action or inaction in the world.

INDEX

Abrams, Meyer, 39-41, 158, 159
"adversary model" of literature, 91, 91n
aesthetics, 155-57 *passim*
affective fallacy, 3
Allegories of Reading (de Man), 115, 172
allegory *vs.* symbol, 118
ambiguity, 3
"Among School Children" (Yeats), 10
amour propre, 59
Anatomy of Criticism (Frye), 4
aphorism, *see* maxim
"appropriation" of text, *see* theft
aristocracy, 81
Aristophanes, 155
Aristotle, 4, 113
Arnold, Matthew, 3-4, 11-12, 16-38 *passim*, 52, 100, 149, 173
Arnold, Thomas, 24
"Arnold as Critic" (Leavis), 20-21
Arnoldian Concordat, 33
atheism, 38, 54
Auerbach, Erich, 103-105
Augustine, St., 40
Austen, Jane, 81, 97
Austin, J. L., 94
author, place of in interpretive community, 98
authority, 8, 21, 78, 82, 85-86, 124, 129, 137
axiom, *see* maxim

Balzac, Honoré de, 47, 49, 65, 74-75, 89
Barth, John, 167
Barthelme, Donald, 166-67
Barthes, Roland, 4, 11, 52, 56-87 *passim*, 88-89, 135, 164, 176
Baudelaire, Charles, 50
Beckett, Samuel, 162-66
"bedrock of belief," 101
belief, 101. *See also* faith
Bellow, Saul, 30n
Bernal, Olga, 166n
Bersani, Leo, 47
biblical criticism, 100-101, 107-108
Birth of Tragedy, The (Nietzsche), 118
Blackmur, R. P., 17n
Bleak House (Dickens), 43
Bleich, David, 109n
Bloom, Harold, 7, 8, 18, 54, 143-44
Boehme, Jacob, 40
Booth, Wayne, 4n
"bourgeois ideology," 69
Bouvard et Pecuchet (Flaubert), 63
Brecht, Bertolt, 67
Broch, Hermann, 50
Brontë, Emily, 43
Brown, Norman O., 155
Burke, Kenneth, 3, 17n, 60, 150-51, 170
Burnett, Ivy Compton, 103

Camus, Albert, 138
Capital (Marx), 56-57
capitalism, 177
Carlyle, Thomas, 23, 29, 41, 56, 111
catharsis, 6
center, 129-30. *See also* authority
Chicago Aristotelians, 4
Christianity, 28, 100-107. *See also* belief; religion

INDEX

coherence, 9, 150
Coleridge, Samuel Taylor, 23
Comédie Humaine, La (Balzac), 47
commodity fetishism, 56, 57, 70
"community," 22
Confessions, The (Rousseau), 121
conservatism, 177
consonance, 119
Coriolanus (Shakespeare), 93, 94
counterculture of 1960s, 18
"Critical Assumption, The," (Culler), 5
"critical power," 34
criticism: biblical, 100-101, 107-108; deconstructive, 111-35 *passim*; "engaged," 179; reader-oriented, 89-95, 106; social, 23, 173-80; as theft, 84, 86
Criticism in the Wilderness (Hartman), 33, 35
Culler, Jonathan, 5-6, 95, 102-103, 134n, 138, 153, 158, 175n
culture, 52; apostolic view of, 36; *vs.* history, 62; literary, 17-20; mass, 71-72
Culture and Anarchy (Arnold), 20, 31, 34-35, 36

"Death of the Author, The," (Barthes), 11, 135
Death of Vergil (Broch), 50
deconstruction, 10, 25-26, 111-35 *passim*; and freedom, 140; and play, 167-68, 171; and social criticism, 173-80
deconstructive "method," 147
deconstructive self, 131-34
deconstructive skepticism, 9-15
Dedalus, Stephen, 48-49, 160-61, 176
degrees of being, 170
de Man, Paul, 112, 135, 168, 174; on deconstructive self, 131-34; on metaphor, 115-22; on Nietzsche and truth, 125-26, 172; on nothingness, 7-8, 25, 37; on the strategy of language, 128
demystification, 9, 56-81 *passim*, 101, 134, 148, 153, 169
Derrida, Jacques, 35, 92, 124n, 134, 135, 141; on difference, 55, 120, 129-31, 137; on criticism as intervention, 144-45, 174-75; on "metaphysical closure," 123-24; on play in language, 165n, 168; on "white mythology," 112-15; on *telos*, 54n-55n, 153-54
desacralization, 26, 28. *See also* secularization
Descartes, René, 12, 131-32
Descombes, Vincent, 134
determinism, 140, 158, 176
dialect, 18
Dickens, Charles, 43
difference (*differance*), 55, 82, 89, 120, 129-31, 135
"disclosure," 153
"dissociation of sensibility," 148n
Dostoevsky, Feodor, 49, 138, 139-40

écriture, 73, 82-83, 87, 89
Eighteenth Brumaire of Louis Bonaparte (Marx), 67
Eliot, George, 12
Eliot, T. S., 2, 3, 17, 18, 21-22, 23, 28, 37-38, 52, 139
Endgame (Beckett), 162-63
Enlightenment, 107
entropy, 147
error, 10, 119
evaluation, 14-15

Failure of Criticism, The (Goodheart), 28n
faith, 10, 162

INDEX

"Fall of Hyperion" (Keats), 40-41
fallacies, 3
Faulkner, William, 97, 98n
Federman, Raymond, 165
"Fehl der Götter" (Hölderlin), 9
Fichte, Johann Gottlieb, 41, 159-60
Finnegans Wake (Joyce), 50, 144
Fischer, Michael, 100
Fish, Stanley, 8, 89-110 *passim*
Flaubert, Gustave, 49, 50, 63
form, 7, 42, 54
Foucault, Michel, 123, 153, 174
France, Anatole, 114
freedom, 54, 90, 109, 110, 140, 152, 154, 158-59, 164, 171, 178
Freud, Sigmund, 61, 72, 131
From Here to Eternity (Jones), 66
Frye, Northrop, 4, 28, 28n, 53-54
"Function of Criticism, The" (Arnold), 33, 34, 36

Gadamer, Hans-Georg, 8-9
games, 161, 162. *See also* play
Garden of Epicurus, The (France), 114
Genesis of Society, The (Kermode), 100
Genet, Jean, 83
Genette, Gerard, 4, 46, 47
genres, theory of (Aristotle), 4
Gide, André, 83
Gnostic Gospels, The (Pagels), 29
Gnosticism, 28-29
Gombrich, E. H., 12n
Goodheart, Eugene, 28n
Graff, Gerald, 12, 12n, 27n
Great Expectations (Dickens), 43
Greece, Classical: *vs.* meaningless present, 42; *vs.* Middle Ages, 23

Hartman, Geoffrey, 25, 33, 34-37 *passim*, 141, 144, 172
healing words, 141
Hegel, Georg Wilhelm Friedrich, 40, 62
Heidegger, Martin, 8, 60, 151-53, 164
Hellenism, 173. *See also* Greece, Classical
Heller, Erich, 49-50, 51
hermeneutics, 83-84, 86
historical context, 99
historical determinism, 176
historical perspective, 98; absence of, 94
history, 16, 62; allied to relativism, 176; *vs.* culture, 62; *vs.* nature, 58; providential, 49
Hölderlin, Friedrich, 9, 41
Holocaust, 30n, 30-31
Homage to Catalonia (Orwell), 177
"home," return to, 44. *See also* transcendental place/site
Homo Ludens (Huizinga), 161
homoiosis, 113
Huizinga, Johann, 155, 161
humanism, 30-31, 151
humanist criticism, 12
Hyperion (Hölderlin), 41

identity, 119. *See also* self
indeterminacy, 86, 87, 102-103, 108, 163
intelligibility, 27, 126, 127
intention, 3, 8, 84-99 *passim*, 137, 145
intentional fallacy, 3
interpretation, 3, 5, 14, 84, 96, 101, 106
interpretive community, 95-102, 107, 109-110
intertextuality, 37
Iser, Wolfgang, 103
Is There a Text in This Class? (Fish), 90, 93n

Jacobinism, 19

Jameson, Fredric, 43-44, 49
Joseph, Gerhard, 18
Joyce, James, 44, 48-49, 50, 52, 144, 176

Kabbalah, 8, 8n
Kafka, Franz, 44
Kazan, Elia, 67
Keats, John, 40-41, 170
Kermode, Frank, 100
Kierkegaard, Søren, 103, 105-106
King Lear (Shakespeare), 6
knowledge: logocentric, 10; subjectivity of, 14
Kramer, Hilton, 16
Krieger, Murray, 10, 33n
Krouse, Michael, 99
Kuhn, Thomas, 99

language, 9, 128; and crime, 75; deceptiveness of, 136; natural, 133; play in, 127, 161-72 *passim*; as system of differences, 120; unconstrained by reality, 74
La Rochefoucauld, François, duc de, 59-60, 68
Lawrence, D. H., 141-43
Leavis, F. R., 3, 17, 20-21
Lenin, V. I., 72-73
Lentricchia, Frank, 168, 172, 174
Letters on the Aesthetic Education of Man (Schiller), 155-57
Leventhal, A. J., 166
Lévi-Strauss, Claude, 145-47, 153
liberalism, 177
linguistics, 55; Saussurean, 76, 120
literature, 63 (*see also* text); "adversary model" of, 91, 91n; deceptiveness of, 80-81; ideological definitions of, 23-24; interpretation of (*see* interpretation); as mimesis, 12-13 (*see also* mimesis); as play, 155-72 *passim*; social purpose of, 27 (*see also* criticism, social); understanding *vs.* experience of, 6
Literature and Dogma (Arnold), 19-20
Literature Against Itself (Graff), 27n
Living Room, The (Greene), 66
logic of organism, 160
Lolita (Nabokov), 170
Lover's Discourse, A (Barthes), 68
Lukács, Georg, 39, 41-44, 49, 157-58

MacDonald, Dwight, 71
Mallarmé, Stéphane, 50
Malone Dies (Beckett), 163
"Man of Letters in the Modern World, The" (Tate), 177
Marcuse, Herbert, 155
Marx, Karl, 56-57, 61, 62, 67, 69-70, 174
Marxism, 175n
Matthew Arnold and American Culture (Raleigh), 21-22
maxim, 68; grammar of, 59-60
meaning, 9, 76, 87, 90, 136-54 *passim*
"Memorial Verses" (Arnold), 149
meta-language, 64
metaphor, 113-18, 124, 148, 150; and guilt, 121; success of, 115
"metaphysical closure," 123
metonymy, 116, 117, 118, 124. *See also* metaphor
Michelangelo, 109n
Miller, J. Hillis, 122, 150, 171
Milton, John, 99
mimesis, 12-13, 46, 113; selective, 49; *vs.* semiosis, 74
Mimesis (Auerbach), 103
miraculism, 53, 112

INDEX

Modern French Philosophy (Descombes), 134
modernism, 71-72
Molloy (Beckett), 163
Morris, William, 23
Morrisette, Bruce, 165n
Moses (Michelangelo), 109n
motive, 105-106
mystification, 32, 145
"Mythologie aujourd'hui, La" (Barthes), 69
Mythologies (Barthes), 56, 58, 63-68, 69
myths, contemporary, 64-67, 68-69

Nabokov, Vladimir, 170
naiveté, 32, 67
narrative, 118, 150
Natural Supernaturalism (Abrams), 39, 159
nature, 119; *vs.* history, 58
ne que, 59-60
néant, 59-60. *See also* nothingness
Negative Capability, 170
New Criticism, 3, 5, 17
New Critics, 37
Nietzsche, Friedrich, 8, 51, 61, 113, 118, 125-26, 172
nihilism, 151
Norris, Christopher, 134n
Notes from Underground (Dostoevsky), 138, 139
nothingness, 7-8, 37, 60, 132, 136, 154, 169, 170
Novalis (Friedrich von Hardenberg), 44

object, *see* subject-object distinction
objectivism, 91, 92
Oedipus, 145-46
On the Waterfront (Kazan), 67
organicism, 157-60
orthodoxy, religious, 23
Orwell, George, 27, 173, 177
ownership of text, 78, 85-86

Pagels, Elaine, 29
paradox, 3; in Barthes, 64-66 *passim*, 79, 87
parody, 64, 78
Paul, St., 19-20
persuasiveness and truth, 101
philistinism, 19
Plato, 133
play in language and literature, 85, 127, 136, 155-72 *passim*
"play impulse," 179
Pleasure of the Text, The (Barthes), 78
pleasure principle, 76
plenitude, 53, 59, 63, 84, 86, 118, 127, 132, 141, 153-60 *passim*, 170, 179
Poetic Presence and Illusion (Krieger), 33n
poetry and religion, 21
Polanyi, Michael, 99
polemic, 92
Popper, Karl, 12n
pornograms, 76
Positions (Derrida), 174
positivism, 36
Poujadism, 67
Pound, Ezra, 18
power, 156
Prelude (Wordsworth), 40-41
presence, 7, 11, 90, 101, 102, 164
Pride and Prejudice (Austen), 81, 97
Prodigal Son, 39-40, 43
projection, 13
proportional sense, 136, 165. *See also* meaning
Proudhon, Pierre-Joseph, 112
Proust, Marcel, 44-48, 52, 83, 115-16, 121

INDEX

"Proust and Names" (Barthes), 76
purposiveness, 127

Raleigh, John, 21-22
randomness, 169
Ransom, John Crowe, 17n, 52-53
rationality, 178
reader-oriented criticism, 89-95, 106
realism, 50, 74
reality principle, 76
reductionism, 60, 61. *See also* demystification
réel vs. vécu, 149
referent, 75n
"referentiality," 27
relativism, 176
religion, 19-25 *passim*, 52; and poetry, 21
Remembrance of Things Past, The (Proust), 44-48, 52
"Replete Literature," 88
"Resistance to Theory, The" (de Man), 133-34
rhetoric, 121
Rhetoric of Fiction (Booth), 4n
Richards, I. A., 3
Ricoeur, Paul, 61, 131
rigor, 126, 128, 129, 131, 155, 172
Rilke, Rainer Maria, 50
Rimbaud, Arthur, 50
Ring Cycle (Wagner), 47
Robbe-Grillet, Alain, 80, 164-65
Roland Barthes by Roland Barthes (Barthes), 58, 68, 83
romanticism, 39-40, 142-43, 149, 159-60
Rorty, Richard, 135
"Rose for Emily, A" (Faulkner), 97, 98n
Rosenberg, Harold, 71, 72
Rousseau, Jean-Jacques, 121-22, 124n
Ruskin, John, 23, 29
Ryan, Michael, 175n

Sade, Donatien, marquis de, 74-76
Sade-Loyola-Fourier (Barthes), 73
Said, Edward, 174
Samson Agonistes (Milton), 99
Sarrasine (Balzac), 65, 77, 79, 89
Sartor Resartus (Carlyle), 19, 41, 111
Sartre, Jean-Paul, 60
Saussure, Ferdinand de, 76, 120
Saving the Text (Hartman), 141, 144
Schiller, Friedrich, 155-57
Scholem, Gershom G., 8
Science and the Modern World (Whitehead), 148
Searle, John, 93n, 94, 168n
secular rationalism, 12
secularization, 19, 23, 108, 111-13
self, 118, 127, 150, 163; deconstructive, 131-34
self-reflexivity, 85
semiosis, 87; *vs.* mimesis, 73-74
semiotics, 72-73, 153
sense, 137-38; propositional, 136, 165
sensibility, 139; dissociation on, 148n; as moral goal, 22
Shakespeare, William, 93, 94, 155
Shelley, Percy Bysshe, 10, 148
significance, 26, 100, 123, 164. *See also* meaning
signifier *vs.* signified, 76-77
skepticism, 106-107, 144, 167, 170, 179-80; anti-theological, 10-11; constitutive, 151; deconstructive, 151; and play, 162
socialism, 177
"society," 16, 22-23
sophistication, 128, 129
Speech Acts: An Essay in the Philosophy

of Language (Searle), 93n
speech-act theory, 93n, 168n
spontaneity, 157
Stambovsky, Phillip A., 105
Stendhal (Marie Henri Beyle), 12, 49
Sterne, Lawrence, 157-58, 161
Stranger, The (Camus), 138
strength, 159
structure, 90, 147; of constraints, 109-110
Structure of Scientific Revolutions, The (Kuhn), 99
structuralism, 4-6, 54, 145-47
"Study of Poetry, The" (Arnold), 20
subject, 14-15, 153
subject-object distinction, 14-15, 91
subjectivism, 109n
subjectivity, 106-107, 152-53
surface, textual, 147
Swann's Way (Proust), 115
symbol *vs.* allegory, 118
S/Z (Barthes), 63, 68, 77, 78-79, 85

Tate, Allen, 17n, 177
teleology, 54-55, 127, 145, 150, 159
telos, 12n, 54, 54n-55n, 137, 145, 154
Teufelsdröckh, Diogenes, 111
text, 7, 17, 37, 80, 95; belief in inherent properties of, 102; multivalent, 77-78; ownership of, 78, 85-86; surface of, 147-48; reinvention of, 83-84
Texts for Nothing (Beckett), 166
texture of the work, 148
theft, criticism as, 84, 86
theme, 124
theory, 26, 134; as demystification, 134; of genres, 4; place of under New Criticism, 3-4; poststructuralist views of, 6-8; and structuralism, 4-6
Theory of the Novel, The (Lukács), 39, 42-44, 49
thereness, 164
thought, 126
To Jerusalem and Back (Bellow), 30n
Todorov, Tzvetan, 4
Tolstoy, Leo, 49, 74-75
totality, 42-43, 52, 54, 77, 87, 88, 107
totalization, 44, 46, 49, 52
Tradition of the New (Rosenberg), 71
transactive model of interpretation, 106
transcendence, 11, 14, 31-38 *passim*, 70
"transcendental homelessness," 41, 43
transcendental space/site, 20, 31-38 *passim*, 39-55 *passim*
transparency of expression, 79
Trilling, Lionel, 17, 18-19, 21-22, 24, 138
"Triumph of Life" (Shelley), 10
tropes, 115, 117, 118, 129, 143
truth, 9, 29, 38, 54, 125, 126, 171, 177; and persuasiveness, 101
"Two Environments, The" (Trilling), 18-19

Ulysses (Joyce), 48-49, 50, 52, 85, 161, 176
"unconcealedness," 153
unity, 120, 155, 157, 161
Unnameable, The (Beckett), 163
utilitarianism, 140

vacuity, 173. *See also* nothingness
Valentinus, 29

INDEX

Valéry, Paul, 50, 161-62
value, 26, 29, 38, 90
values, 110, 126, 128, 152, 175
vécu vs. réel, 149
void, 163. *See also* nothingness

Wagner, Richard, 47
Waiting for Godot (Beckett), 164
"welter of implication," 103
"What is Criticism?" (Barthes), 84-85
White, Hayden, 51-52
"White Mythology" (Derrida), 113
Whitehead, Alfred North, 148-49
will, 107, 118, 127, 128, 143-45
will-to-know, 144
will-to-make-sense, 128
will-to-truth, 128
Williams, Raymond, 17
Women in Love (Lawrence), 141-43
Wordsworth, William, 27, 40-41, 148
wounding words, 141
Writing and Difference (Derrida), 54n-55n
Writing Degree Zero (Barthes), 79
Wuthering Heights (Brontë), 43

Yeats, William Butler, 10

PRINCETON ESSAYS IN LITERATURE

January 1984

The Orbit of Thomas Mann.
By Erich Kahler

On Four Modern Humanists: Hofmannsthal, Gundolf, Curtius, Kantorowicz.
Edited by Arthur R. Evans, Jr.

Flaubert and Joyce: The Rite of Fiction.
By Richard Cross

A Stage for Poets: Studies in the Theatre of Hugo and Musset.
By Charles Affron

Hofmannsthal's Novel "Andreas."
By David H. Miles

Kazantzakis and the Linguistic Revolution in Greek Literature.
By Peter Bien

Modern Greek Writers.
Edited by Edmund Keeley and Peter Bien

On Gide's "Prométhée": Private Myth and Public Mystification.
By Kurt Weinberg

The Inner Theatre of Recent French Poetry: Cendrars; Tzara, Peret, Artaud, Bonnefoy.
By Mary Ann Caws

Wallace Stevens and the Symbolist Imagination.
By Michel Benamou

Cervantes' Christian Romance: A Study of "Persiles y Sigismunda."
By Alban K. Forcione

The Prison-House of Language:
A Critical Account of Structuralism and Russian Formalism.
By Fredric Jameson

Ezra Pound and the Troubadour Tradition.
By Stuart Y. McDougal

Wallace Stevens: Imagination and Faith.
By Adalaide K. Morris

On the Art of Medieval Arabic Literature.
By Andras Hamori

The Poetic World of Boris Pasternak.
By Olga Hughes

The Aesthetics of György Lukács.
By Béla Királyfalvi

The Echoing Wood of Theodore Roethke.
By Jenijoy La Belle

Achilles' Choice: Examples of Modern Tragedy.
By David Lenson

The Figure of Faust in Valéry and Goethe.
By Kurt Weinberg

The Situation of Poetry: Contemporary Poetry and Its Traditions.
By Robert Pinsky

The Symbolic Imagination: Coleridge and the Romantic Tradition.
By J. Robert Barth, S.J.

Adventures in the Deeps of the Mind:
The Cuchulain Cycle of W. B. Yeats.
By Barton R. Friedman

Shakespearean Representation:
Mimesis and Modernity in Elizabethan Tragedy.
By Howard Felperin

René Char: The Myth and the Poem.
By James R. Lawler

The German Bildungsroman from Wieland to Hesse.
By Martin Swales

Six French Poets of Our Time: A Critical and Historical Study.
By Robert W. Greene

Coleridge's Metaphors of Being.
By Edward Kessler

The Lost Center and Other Essays in Greek Poetry.
By Zissimos Lorenzatos

Shakespeare's Revisions of "King Lear."
By Steven Urkowitz

Coleridge on the Language of Verse.
By Emerson Marks

The Figure of Dante: An Essay on "The Vita Nuova."
By Jerome Mazzaro

The Image of the City in Modern Literature.
By Burton Pike

The Imaginary Library: An Essay on Literature and Society.
By Alvin B. Kernan

Pope's "Iliad": Homer in the Age of Passion.
By Steven Shankman

LIBRARY OF CONGRESS CATALOGING IN PUBLICATION DATA

Goodheart, Eugene.
The skeptic disposition in contemporary criticism.

(Princeton essays in literature)
Includes index.
1. Deconstruction. 2. Skepticism. 3. Criticism—History—20th century. I. Title. II. Series.
PN98.D43G66 1984 801'.95 84-15076
ISBN 0-691-06626-4 (alk. paper)

Eugene Goodheart is Edytha Macy Gross Professor of Humanities at Brandeis University. He is the author of *The Utopian Vision of D. H. Lawrence* (Chicago, 1963), *The Cult of the Ego: The Self in Modern Literature* (Chicago, 1968), *Culture and the Radical Conscience* (Harvard, 1973), and *The Failure of Criticism* (Harvard, 1978).

GPSR Authorized Representative: Easy Access System Europe - Mustamäe tee 50, 10621 Tallinn, Estonia, gpsr.requests@easproject.com

www.ingramcontent.com/pod-product-compliance
Ingram Content Group UK Ltd.
Pitfield, Milton Keynes, MK11 3LW, UK
UKHW021855060725
460447UK00004B/407

* 9 7 8 0 6 9 1 6 1 1 9 0 7 *